HANDS

Tara Hands

ISBN Number 1-57087-142-6

Professional Press
Chapel Hill, NC 27515-4371

Manufactured in the United States of America
96 95 94 93 92   10 9 8 7 6 5 4 3 2 1

Dedication

This book is dedicated to single women travelers, both famous and otherwise, who have motivated me, such as Nellie Bly, who went around the world in 72 days via horse, boat, and train in 1889. Polly, my five-week companion in 1985, and Amber, an enthusiast of the Orient, and Margaret, a Central American volunteer, and Edee, my six-week companion in 1990, and Laurene, a six-year mobile (recreational vehicle) home traveler, and Darlene, a winner of various challenges.

Credit must also be given to my mother who encouraged my risk taking and to the Unity Church which inspired positive attitudes. I cannot omit the Quaker faith which enhanced my willingness to live quietly and simply. To my Creator, I acknowledge the gifts of health, money and curiosity—to see, to ask, and to share.

Tara Hands
Honolulu, Hawaii

Reading Thoughts

Biography

These recollected experiences have influenced my thoughts, aided in my skills development and given me some interesting interpretations about what I have seen.

I was born in Bedford, Ohio, a suburb of Cleveland. I lived in a loving home with an older and a younger brother, and then a sister when I was 15. Two years of secretarial training at Stephens College in Missouri, along with a spring vacation trip to Cuba with a touring college group in 1952, followed by a summer and two years of office work in Honolulu, may have ignited my urge to travel.

During a marriage to an audio-visual artist which lasted nineteen years, we adopted two brothers who were 8 and 10. They now live with their spouses in Oregon and New York. Cancer appeared in my life 20 years ago and I was given a 50-50 chance of survival. Three medical sessions after the two surgeries, I gave up the treatments and allowed my body to heal on its own without any change in diet or activities.

During 25 years of public school teaching in Honolulu, my extra energy was given to workshops, club meetings,

University classes, Erhart Seminar Training, Toastmasters, Adventures in Attitudes, and PSI Mind Development. Volunteer work included the YWCA, local community projects, serving as co-chair of the local chapter of the Campaign for a national Peace Tax Fund and Educators for Social Responsibility, plus writing letters to local newspapers.

After being single for ten years, I took my first trip to Europe in 1985 with Polly for five weeks. I then continued for five months alone visiting schools in Austria, Italy, Switzerland, France, Ireland, Wales, Scotland, England, India, Thailand, Australia and New Zealand.

During the summer of 1986 I attended summer school in Vancouver, BC, Canada, and volunteered at the World's Fair held there. In 1988 I won a fellowship for six-weeks of study at the University of South Carolina. First I traveled to the Caribbean, and after the course, I went across the United States by bus. In 1990 I spent the entire year on a Professional Improvement Leave without pay from the Hawaii Department of Education to visit schools in 32 countries. That great adventure follows.

Introduction

These articles are not intended to be anything except what they are—a simple presentation of observations about schools, classes, towns, conversations and countries as seen and heard through the eyes of this global wandering and wondering educator. I believe that many teachers, parents and travelers would love to have a brief glimpse of the educational practices and traditions that occur throughout the world.

This collection of articles gives my own response to some of the challenges of education. This information is presented in the spirit of sharing and encouraging others to travel. I hope you will enjoy them as much as I did observing these events.

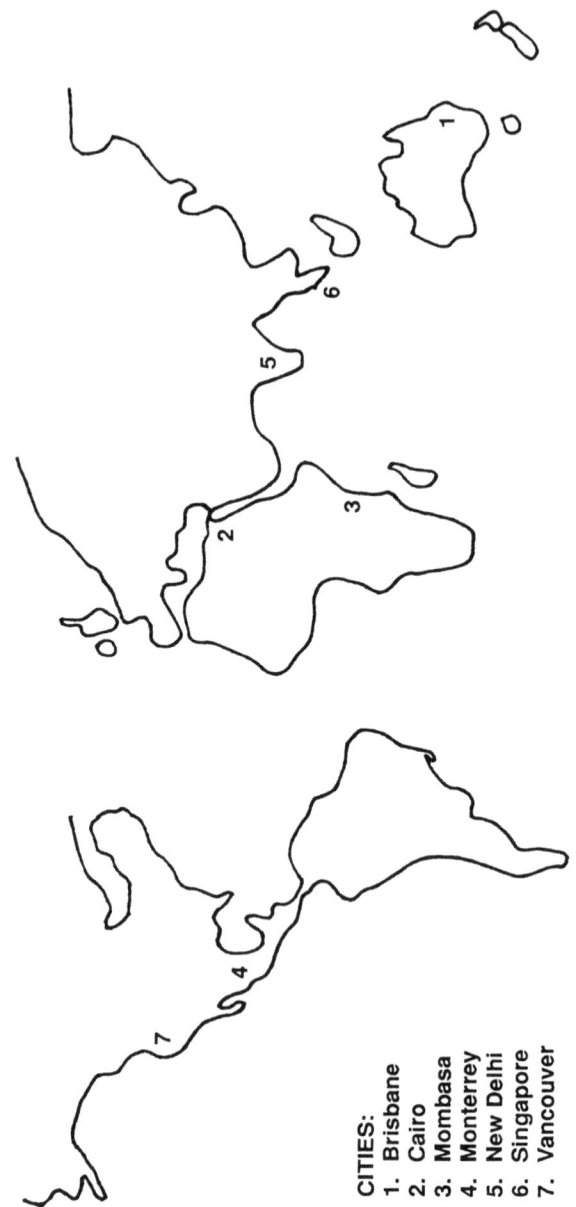

CITIES:
1. Brisbane
2. Cairo
3. Mombasa
4. Monterrey
5. New Delhi
6. Singapore
7. Vancouver

Map of the World

Index

These page numbers are marked for easy reference to information and country.

Map of the World 8
Travel Adventure Plans 15
Map of South Asia 20
Taiwan 21
Hong Kong 24
Canton (Guangzhou), PRC 27
Macau 31
Singapore 34
Malaysia 37
Indonesia 41
Brunei 43
Bangkok, Thailand 47
Cairo, Egypt 51
Map of West Europe 55
Athens, Greece 56
Map of Italy 60
Rome, Italy 61
Florence And Southern Italy 66
Haiku Poetry................................69
The Adriatic Riviera 82
Bassano Del Grappa, Italy 86
Bolzano, Italy 89
Innsbruck, Austria 92
Munich, Germany 94
Oberammergau, Germany 98

Garmisch, Germany 102
Vaduz, Liechtenstein 104
Luxembourg City, Luxembourg 109
Brugge, Belgium 112
Tourcoing, France 115
Ghent, Belgium 119
Amsterdam, Netherlands 123
Utrecht, Netherlands 126
Copenhagen and Frederickshavn, Denmark 129
Oslo, Norway 133
Northern Norway 137
Central Finland 140
Southern Finland 144
St. Petersburg, Russia 147
Sweden 151
Western Berlin, Germany 155
Eastern Berlin, Germany 158
Bedford, England 163
Stratford-On-Avon, England 168
Kenya, East Africa 171
Bedford, Ohio, USA 176
Georgetown, Texas, USA 179
Monterrey, Mexico 183
Vancouver, British Columbia 185
A Series Of Travelers' Prayers 189
Expenditures For Education By Country 191
Memories of 1985 193
1985 Country Comments 198
Author's Final Thoughts 217
School Addresses 219
Photographs 223, 224

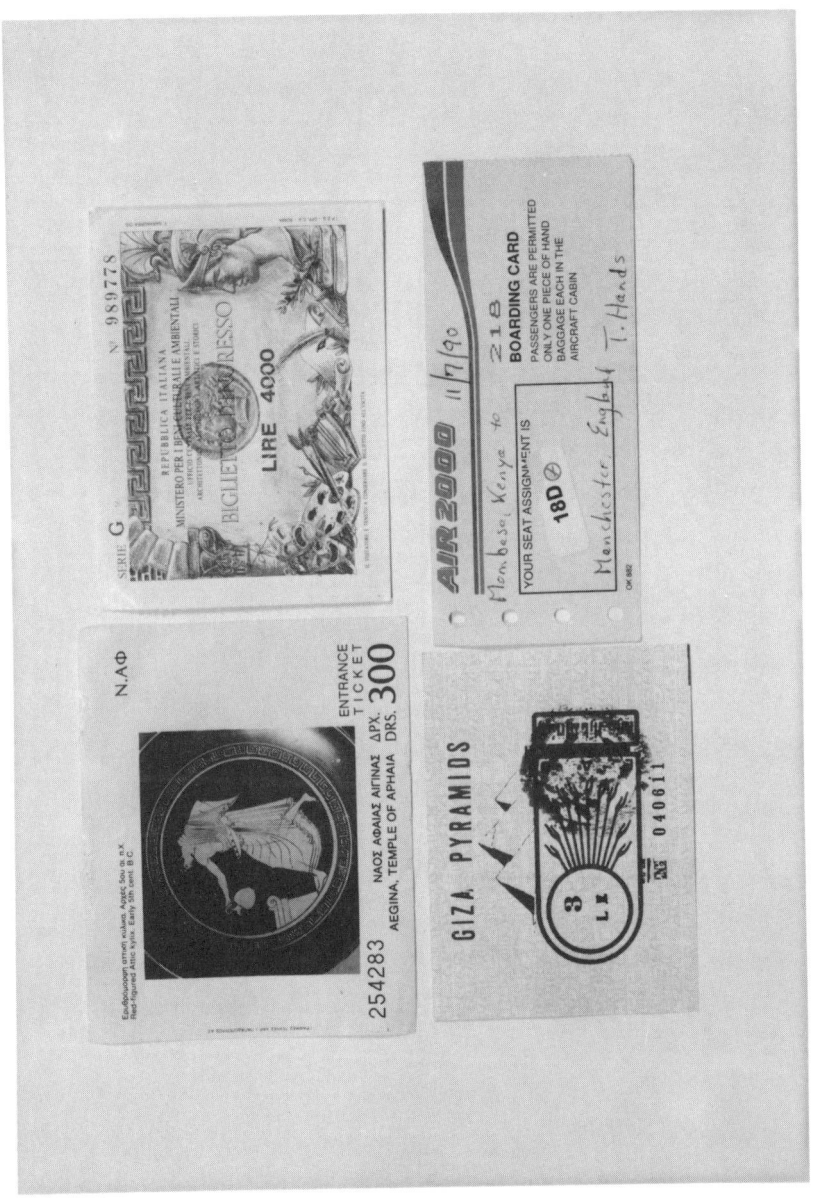

Museum Tickets

Collection of Stones

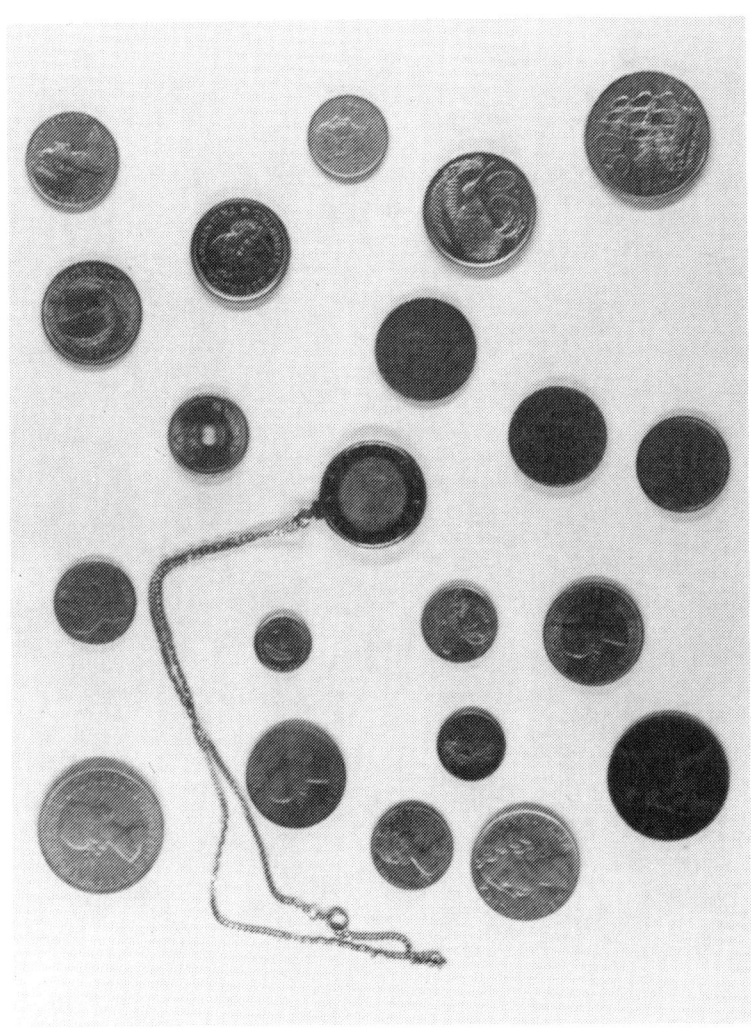

Coins

Paper Money

Travel Adventure Plans

November 12, 1989

What a great idea—traveling around the world with a friend! I was planning to visit schools along the way as I had on my first adventure in 1985 for six months. Capturing the spirit of education in words this time would be quite special as the suburban "Sun Press" newspaper in Honolulu had agreed to publish these articles. My mind and heart had begun working on ways to make this westward trek which was to last seven to twelve months, depending on the amount of money, energy and interest that could be made to last. I would be able to borrow money from a sheltered annuity, take a professional improvement leave of absence from my public school elementary teaching duties, and get a friend to handle the local details after my departure. The sooner I made the decision to travel, the more time I would have for the necessity of planning.

The details of planning to be away from home for a year while traveling through 32 countries is a major undertaking. Allowing two months for planning adds deadlines and decisions concerning personal inner questions and reflections. Some of the personal "nitty-gritty" details involve plans to grant someone a power of attorney, an up-to-date will, a notarized paper to carry concerning death overseas, storing personal items, selling or keeping (where?) one's automobile, the maintaining or evacuating one's home, the early filing of the year's income tax papers, and handling checks, papers and mail.

Some of the first travel steps are to obtain wallet-size photos needed for visas to other countries and a passport. Travel agencies can give you details as to what is needed where. Questions need to be written down with the name and phone number of the person who answers. Helpful page titles in a notebook for planning are: questions (with space for answers & dates), steps to complete, people to see, items and clothes to take, addresses & phone numbers, follow up information, airline comparisons, and local details.

In 1985 I traveled for six months on a $2000 ticket around the world with Thailand, SAS and United Air Lines. In 1990 the fare was still $2000 but now good for one year with a choice of two airlines. We chose American and Singapore Airlines. This fare allows an unlimited number of stopovers. Make a list of countries that you plan to visit. Check with a travel agency and call the various airlines free 800 number to verify that you are proceeding in one direction (no backtracking allowed) and that the plane does go from your destination to your next choice. This phase is most important and time consuming. Looking at an airline's timetable, globes and maps will still not complete the process accurately. The airlines "rate desk" informs the travel agency which cities are not included in the special fare. Even though one is allowed to travel without committing to certain dates, each city must be ticketed. This list of cities should then be presented to your local physician to determine the need for any inoculations or medicines associated with the planned itinerary.

The public library's travel section will often provide considerable amounts of information. Recording data into a travel notebook (shorthand pad) by country headings is valuable upon arriving. Special sites to see, people to visit, weather facts, places to stay, currency values, etc. are invaluable resources as locating a library phone book, book stores, etc. can be very time consuming in a strange location.

The amount of money to carry is a challenge. Plastic charge cards are accepted world-wide. Two are recommended. I had one, but only had trouble in Paris. Travelers checks are good for emergencies but they are too bulky for long term travels. Banks offer the best currency exchange rates. Obtaining $20 of the local currency for each foreign destination before arriving there is a great confidence asset for taxi, tips, and snacks. Exchange desks may not be open at the train station or airport. Local coins are another matter. The best way to obtain these is to purchase some item at the airport shop to get coins for phoning for room reservations, and tipping. Carrying a calculator will help you in comparing the cost of everything in your money vs. the present country. The receipt given when exchanging money will give you the rate of exchange. Remember to find out in advance how many local bills need to be saved for the departure airport tax.

Another major task is to pack everything into one carry-on bag to avoid lost luggage. In 1985 I was able to do this and placed the dufflebag under the plane seat; however, today the planes seem to have less room (seat pitch is now down to 29" in some airlines). Valuable items and papers should be hand-carried. Money belts and/ or neck purses for passports, checks, cards, etc. are a necessary humbug.

A great service was a free phone call from travels to the NEA-Master Charge Card department in Delaware once a month. My friend Sandy would call that number on the 10th with my bank balance and answers to questions that I had written. I'd call on the 12th for my messages.

Being single again for the past fifteen years offered flexibility and opportunity to take advantage of special situations. Some people prefer to travel with the company of an organized tour, while others prefer to travel alone or with a friend. This planned trip with so many destinations and for such a long time was cheaper with a partner and making one's own plans. Traveling with one to share the hotel costs and delights of the day is often preferred if the two people are able to handle communication problems, privacy time, and personality traits. Often traveling involves more togetherness time than a marriage. Situations for negotiations arise regularly. The advantages of the travel tours are that someone does all your planning, thinking and general expensing The advantage of solo adventures are having more control over when and where you go, what you do, and how much you spend for basics as lodging and food. As a soloist you can choose each minute to continue or change directions without having to explain. As with every situation, and choice, there are drawbacks and advantages.

During the planning process the question will arise—
"Why are you doing this? and especially for me, "Why,
again?" The sales line, "See the world before you leave it,"
was a very powerful advertisement for a local travel
agency. It reminded me that every place in the world had
something special to offer, something special to experience. People have that unique quality too. Travel gives
you the chance to concentrate on the surprises of new
conversations, different scenery, and unusual events.
Opening your eyes in a place you have never seen before
creates a special feeling for the pleasures of the unknown.
Perhaps this explains why once around the world is not
enough.

In 1985 when I was traveling, I distributed rainbow-
colored pens that read, "Think, live, and work for peace."
In 1990, I took 750 Earth Seal stickers. The picture shown
on the seal was the now-famous photograph taken during
the Apollo XVII flight to the moon in 1972 (order from
Gala, Box 8000, Berkeley, Calif.). This would encourage
me to initiate a conversation daily and remind me of the
need to look beyond nationalities. Teaching 28 years in
various public schools has made me curious about what
is happening in other classrooms.

A Bloom County Cartoon (1985): "On your feet, brave
knave... adventure awaits! Time is short and the world is
vast, young knight...hurry! We have much to do and see!
Fantastic horizons! Enchanted Kingdoms, Magical Lands
beyond imagination with chocolate dragons and white-
satin maidens who look like "Madonna" with her hair
combed! So hop on up, lad! There's a whole life-time of
meaningful personal discovery ahead of us!"

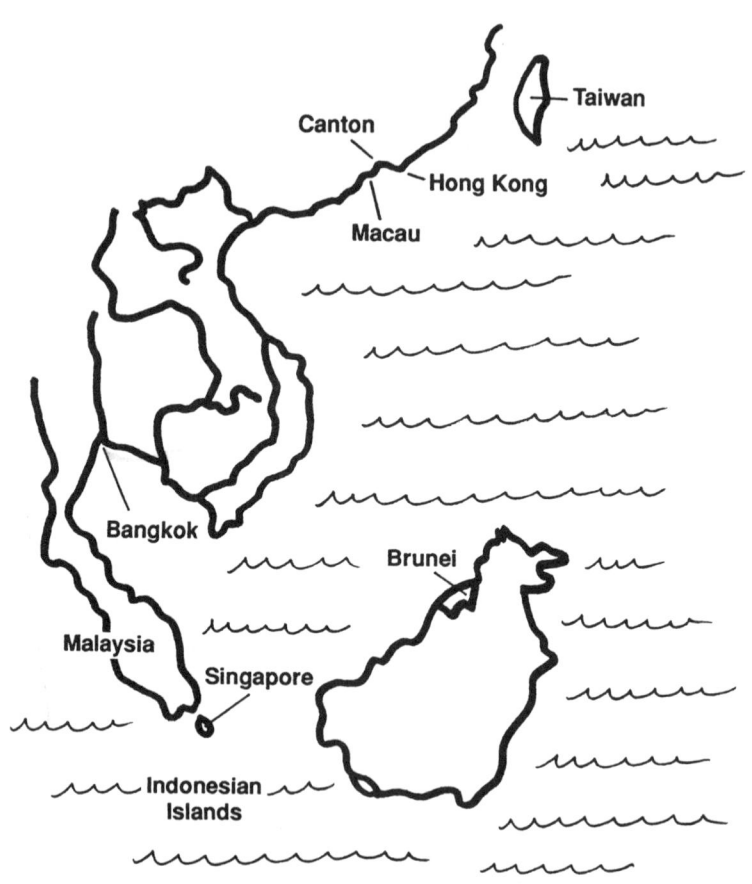

Map of South Asia

Taiwan

January 8, 1990

C hung Sing Primary School is about a 15-minute walk from the railway station in Taipei, Taiwan. Six-hundred boys and girls from grades 1 through 6 wear blue jackets, white shirts, and blue pants in this U-shaped, three-story typical building. Classes begin at 8 a.m. and run until 4:10 p.m., including Saturdays until noon. The children begin the day by standing at attention in the courtyard for morning announcements and then proceed to self-contained classrooms of 34 students each. Students sit side-by-side in pairs in every room.

I met with the principal of the school who was also a sixth grade teacher. She introduced me to an energetic, rapid English-speaking fourth grade male teacher of physical education, music, mathematics, and writing. We bounded up to the second floor to his students who were eating candy snacks and sharing items in celebration of a monthly birthday party for classmates. Two students brought us hard chocolate candies.

Various class writings were posted on the back display board. A six-inch brush pen dipped in a tray of hard ink, mixed later with water, is the primary writing instrument. Homework is a daily 30-minute task that often includes such assignments as visiting a museum, helping one's parents, reviewing work, and writing activities. English is not offered before secondary school. Marks are given ranging from A to D, but the six yearly exams are scored by points.

Percy Chiu, my fourth-grade teacher and guide, indicated that in Taiwan, all males at 21 must complete two years of military service. Chiu, himself, then went on to complete four years of Normal College (teacher's college). Junior and senior high school teachers go to the National University of Taiwan. Teachers usually get a small yearly salary increase. Presently the salary is $1,112 monthly. Parents must pay $32 per semester for public schooling while private schooling costs about $400 per semester.

Slow learners are tutored individually with a teacher sitting across from the student's desk. In the session I visited, only two students and two teachers were in the room. In another room, twelve mentally handicapped children were being taught basics of personal care: making the bed in the room and preparing food. Two teachers were working in this large room which was equipped with special supplies.

In Taiwan, there is no government-subsidized welfare program. Relatives are encouraged to help out with the routine school expenses of lunches, books, and clothing. Most parents in the Chung Sing Primary School area are in business.

My own experiences with these children included a high-speed bus ride to and down into a magnificent gorge—this is one of Asia's highlights with shrines, water-falls, and narrow mountain passes. A 12-year-old girl gave me her candy bar. On the way back, one of the ten teenage girls with us gave us an orange and sweet green popcorn. Youths here seem to be more willing than adults to extend hospitality.

What I'll remember most about Taiwan is the thousands of motor scooters dodging the cars, driving onto the sidewalks of the park, and whizzing around walkers in the crosswalks. The Grand Hotel is truly grand, while Chiang Kai-Shek Memorial Hall is definitely memorable, and the Hualien Gorge is exceptionally gorgeous!

Hong Kong

January 12, 1990

I s there a King Kong in Hong Kong? Children at Peniel School would be unable to answer right away as English is not taught to these cute youngsters of ages 3, 4, and 5.

There are 14 teachers for the nine classes of Chinese students, each wearing their bright red jackets. Half of the students come to school at 9 a.m. and leave at noon. The other half attends from 1 to 4 p.m. The school at one time served older children but changed its venue to serve this need.

The school is located on Portland Street. When we arrived, we saw that the building's lights were on, but were unable to get in until a parent came out with her child at around 9:30 a.m. There is a button on the right wall inside the gate, but its use was unknown to us. We saw no one as we walked up to the nondenominational Christian church sanctuary where students were being dismissed. Up six flights of stairs, we followed a class of 34 students who sat at 18" x 12" tables facing each other in three U-shaped groups.

The teacher then passed out a reading readiness booklet which was placed in the students' 10-inch red shopping bag for homework. After instructions were given, one group placed their chairs in a row. When all of the children were squeezed in rows between the tables, she left us alone with them for a few moments.

The principal (a woman) and an English-speaking, friendly teacher arrived and began to tell us about the Hong Kong schools. High school graduate teachers are given three months' training by the local department of education and make about $326 monthly. Families pay about $26 monthly for Monday through Friday schooling of their children. Parents help with picnics or educational excursions, and meet with teachers for semester conferences and at group meetings.

We observed several classes on the roof at recess time, riding tricycles and swinging horizontally on a group board. Downstairs was a large indoor physical education area with students sitting by the walls waiting for their turn to use beanbags and rocking horses.

Children, living in the Peniel School area, live in an area of continuous construction and welding. Yet the neighborhood virtually teems with fruit sellers, hardware stores, equipment stores, and dinner food carts and tables set up between sidewalks. All the buildings in the Pitt Street area location seemed to be of seven stories with solid metal gates covering inside shops at night. Two streets away is Nathan Street which has the second most expensive storefront property in the world ($550 per square foot—Tokyo's Ginza brings $675).

Hong Kong planned to build 20 more new hotels in

1990. It competes for tourist money with Singapore and Thailand. Apartment flats of from 560 to 790 square feet were sold during the month I visited Hong Kong for a minimum price of $96,000. Yiu Wing Construction Holdings, Ltd., sold all 150 units in Happy Valley on its first January marketing day.

While I was waiting on the street for a bus, six teenaged girls gave me a questionnaire written in English. It contained ten questions and asked what did I think of the food, the people, the traffic, the sights. The girls didn't speak English, but seemed pleased to get a completed form and an Earth sticker from me. I did state that I liked the modern architecture of the four major bank buildings.

We took the mass rapid transit system to the university to visit the art gallery. The following notice was on the counter with a donation box:

"Members of the Teachers Association (CUTA) and Staff Association (CUSA) of the Chinese University of Hong Kong have joined together and organized themselves into 'the Association' to fight for the ideals of freedom, democracy, and basic human rights in alliance with all other patriotic democratic groups in Hong Kong and throughout the world"

The double-decker buses are a 20-cent treat to use to notice kindergartens located in the second story of downtown stores. Most of these stores sell shoes, jewelry, or clothing.

Canton (Guangzhou), PRC
January 15, 1990

Getting to Canton (known here as Guangzhou) involves a 30-minute rapid-transit ride from Hong Kong to the Chinese frontier and then a scenic two-and-a-half-hour train ride. About 500 people rush off and squeeze you through the passport checks once you arrive. We waited until the end of the crush, hoping to avoid the crowd, but we got caught in the next trainload that arrived at 9:30 a.m. We then had considerable difficulty locating the local train station. Fortunately, the clerk at the station where we were refused to sell us any tickets, and a policeman directed us to the proper window. In retrospect, it was worth enduring being squashed and rushed at the border station to finally be able to sit on a slow Chinese train and to drink authentic Chinese tea.

We listened to piped-in local music while observing drizzle-covered vegetable fields and concrete two-story, fifty-yard-wide structures with seventeen horizontal windows. I saw only a handful of people wearing gray plastic, hooded ponchos on bicycles on the roads beside the railroad tracks.

I was a bit nervous about this particular journey since the Hong Kong papers had indicated that some thirty people had been executed the week prior to my arrival. A teacher had also been sentenced to ten years in jail for displaying a slogan that attacked the Chinese leadership. However, this day, all was quiet in the 50°F weather, even though the city was quite crowded. Our hotel had nine restaurants and room "freebies" of slippers, combs, shampoo, foam bath soap, shower cap, toothbrushes, and toothpaste—it cost only $40 per night.

Local television programming was quite entertaining, especially the commercials—a bowling ball smashes into a mattress while the sleeping girl barely moves; a bride and groom hang out of a helicopter to have bus passengers catch the bridal bouquet; an inchworm slowly crawls up a leaf and the camera pans to a shot of toothpaste. The five local channels gave out 15 second commercials selling ties, luggage, slow cookers (for rice, etc.), children singing and dancing to the "Twinkle, Twinkle, Little Star" song then cheering for candy. One program featured elementary students looking at a green chalkboard with a clock above it in the center (a scene typical of most American classrooms). Blue-jacketed high school students sat one to a desk. Children were observing other children write on individual tables at a park. A group of ten-year-olds in red and white uniforms were blowing 8-inch metal harmonicas; the instruments had a second keyboard on the side. It sounded a lot like an accordion. The program then concluded with three second flashes of each previous commercial.

Even though I had the request, "Please show me to a child education school," written in Chinese, no one in our hotel seemed to know where one was located. Later, when I was chatting with a woman named Judy at our hostel in Hong Kong, I would learn that she had joined a Pennsylvania Mennonite group to work with student nurses in China. She worked six months in the interior city of Quong Ching which has a population of 12,000,000 living in a heavily polluted environment. Classes at the various schools started 8:00 a.m. and continued until noon with a break until 2:30 p.m. Then school would resume and continue to 5:30 p.m.

Fourth graders studied algebra, science, and pinyin (writing letters from Chinese characters). The cement school that Judy observed needed repair. Its windows were broken; there was no central heating. There were 40 students in a class along with a teacher and a teacher's aid. Fifteen hundred students attended grades one through six and wore no uniforms.

Art projects were created from refuse; pictures were made from pencil shavings and carvings were done in chalk. Girls at age fifteen are chosen on the basis of their grades to enter a three-year nursing program. Nursing is quite specialized, thus most of Judy's training was not utilized. She lectured and listened when the translator spoke. Others working in China had the same assignment—teach English.

The China Reconstructs magazine, December 1989, printed Philip Gottling's (a musician in the Honolulu symphony) article entitled "Teaching Music, Learning about China." And, excerpted from *Development of*

China magazine, "In April 1986, the National People's Congress [of China] passed a compulsory nine-years educational law for free education. In 1988, there were 1,071,000 schools at all levels in urban and rural areas with 1,075 colleges of higher learning."

Macau

January 17, 1990

How now, Macau? Where art thou? It is a one-hour jet foil ride of about 65 kilometers (40 miles) southwest from Hong Kong. Macau is a pleasant change from 30-story apartment buildings, banks, and shops. The main sections of this Portuguese colony are on the coast with bridges and buses connecting the two nearby southern islands by another one-hour ride. It is interesting to note that the Portuguese colony was attacked by the Dutch, the Spanish, the French, the English, the Chinese, the Japanese, and pirates throughout its history.

Our search for a nearby elementary school began. Some employees of the Lisboa Hotel tried to give us directions to the school; however, many were unaware that it was only a block away.

The Santa Rosa de Lima English Primary School has 1,180 students in grades kindergarten through six. The fifth and sixth grade classes consist of girls only. Forty-six children were in each of the kindergarten classes. The day began at 8:15 a.m. and ran until noon. At 2:00 p.m. classes resumed and lasted until 4:00 p.m. Only ten students remained at the school during the lunch break from noon to 2 p.m. The school year runs from September to June with a weeks' holiday at Christmas and two weeks' holiday for the Chinese New Year in February. Classes contain students of mixed abilities. Those having difficulty are pulled out for counseling or remedial classes. Catholic students are given religious instruction three times weekly while others are taught ethics. Grades one through six have computer classes and lessons in Cantonese.

The faculty of the school consisted of teachers of Filipino, Indian, and Chinese nationalities. Macau also receives Hong Kong graduates from the Chinese Normal Training Programs. The Macau East Asian College also cooperates with Hong Kong by providing a two-year educational program. Teachers are usually employed in the mornings and attend classes in the afternoons for a period of two years. Parents rarely assist in the classrooms, but do attend two evening programs of two hours each. Homework is assigned daily. Report cards are sent home five times per school year. There are three school terms with a charge of $100 per term.

The kindergarten students I photographed were standing quietly in line with the teacher at her desk to begin the procession to the inner courtyard to greet waiting parents. Three helmets were put on as both parents took their child home on a motorcycle. Many parents worked nights at the various casinos and greyhound racetracks. Gambling has been legal in Macau since 1962.

From the tourist's point of view, I enjoyed the Hyatt

Hotel. They served coffee with a three-tier pedestal tray of fruit, pastry, and sandwiches to enjoy with piano music in the lobby. The view of the arching bridge and Macau (which means city of God) from the island of Taipa is relaxing in spite of the traffic. The hotel van takes you to the ferry and casinos where one-third of the country's income is generated. The Portuguese government appoints a governor for the 95% Chinese population located on this 15 sq. km. area on the southern peninsula of China. It should also be noted that while Hong Kong will be returned to China in 1997, there is no treaty between Portugal and China to restore Macau to China.

Singapore

January 22, 1990

The Singapore Life Church Kindergarten employs 13 teachers that serve approximately 150 students aged three to six. These children are taught English from 9 a.m. until noon. Along with English, the government insists that Mandarin (Chinese) be the second language taught in the schools. This practice began in the late 1960s. Many Japanese parents pay extra to the school to allow their children to remain until 2 p.m. Most of the students take a bus from the suburbs with grandparents or with Filipino or Indian maids.

The schools in Singapore have undergone considerable change. Singapore's elementary schools have moved out to the suburban area of the city. About half of Singapore's kindergarten's are run by churches. Independent schools have increased fees from S$10 monthly to S$100 monthly. High school students wear uniforms and long ties.

The facilities at Singapore Life Church Kindergarten were impressive. Children were climbing on creative wood structures, had a tiled figure-eight water play table, had enclosed learning rooms, and had an open-walled movement area. Children were clapping and singing in three languages with the piano instructor. I visited with two teachers who served a morning snack of iced cookies and watered orange drink.

The principal of the school had spent a week in Hawaii on the island of Oahu. He showed me the report card booklet that was sent home twice a year. Two colored photographs of children in action were on each of the six pages. As I left the grounds of the school I met a minister who spoke Cantonese. He shares the church with the Presbyterians.

At one of the many food courts along the street nearby, I met a man from Vermont who had just attended a well-known school here, the "Regional English Language Center." This center gives an 8-week course in teaching conversational English and English grammar. The courses usually run from May through June and from November through December. The Vermonter and his Canadian wife had taught school in China. They indicated that if one would sign a contract to teach when away from home, one could obtain about 30% more pay. Anyone with a degree willing to teach English will find work in Asia.

While I visited Singapore, I made note of some of the headlines in *The Straits Times*: "Indonesia totally prohibits smoking in schools," "A Singapore motorcyclist crashes and kills a 15-year-old school girl" (his sentence was four months in jail and a five-year driving ban), "A $12 dance party for 6,000 youths will be held from 7:30 p.m. to 2:30 a.m. at the Westin Hotel," "The new $6 million secondary St. Gabriel School is designed in the shape of the Chinese character for heaven." Singapore is as diverse as any international city could hope to be.

Once a part of the British Commonwealth of Nations, Singapore was overrun by the Japanese in 1942. In 1963, the island was a part of the Federation of Malaysia. In 1990, Singapore celebrated 25 years as an independent republic. The republic is served by 47 foreign missions, 38 banks, 51 international airlines with 14 million passengers annually, and 5 million tourists that arrive by other means make this 573 sq. km. located 1° north of the Equator the crossroads of the world.

Malaysia

January 31, 1990

Jahore Bahru is located on the southern tip of the Malay Peninsula. A one-hour bus ride for S$2 crosses a bridge to leave the Singapore island. At the time I made this trek, 13 Malay dollars (pink) equaled 10 Singapore dollars (also pink) which equaled 5 American dollars (green).

Just a five-minute walk from the bus stop puts one on a street without sidewalks that goes by ten schools. The first school, Holy Light Kindergarten, was on vacation so I trudged up the hill to Mengapa Tunassusi (Tadika Islam) School which was developed ten years ago by a 74-year old school teacher.

This woman solicited funds to build the four classrooms, administration office, kitchen, one-bed sick room, and stage-auditorium (which has no seating). There are 42 kindergarten students in two different classes. Teachers earn about M$200 monthly and teach classes from 8:30 -11:30 a.m. daily. The school, itself, receives no governmental support. Parents of Islamic faith pay M$30 monthly for tuition.

The spacious classrooms had round tables, toys, mats, ceiling fans, and number and alphabet posters in both English and Arabic. The English booklets dealt with letter formation and mathematics along with letter formation. Students would copy from these.

The school year runs from December to October. Grades one through six are offered at the school where boys wear caps and girls that sit apart from the boys wear head scarves. Lessons are taught in Arabic, Malay, and English.

After departing Mengapa Tunassusi, I visited Sekolah RJK (C) St. Joseph School. It has 1,365 Chinese students aged 7 through 12 and employs 48 teachers. Each teacher has from 40 to 50 students in a class and rotates class-rooms during sessions. Students are of both genders and generally of Chinese-Malaysian ancestry. Depending on their educational level teachers can earn from M$550 to M$2,000 monthly.

There are no school fees, but textbooks cost M$40 - M$70 per year. The school uniform costs M$15. All of Malaysia's schools require the same blue and white clothing colors for primary students. Teachers and students come to class in one term from 7:30 a.m. to 12:15 p.m. The next term they would come to class from 1:00-6:20 p.m. Lessons are taught in Mandarin, Malay, and English. Church brothers teach scripture once a week to some 20% of the student body who have shown interest in this study. Secondary school lessons are taught in Malay. English is a compulsory second language.

In 1989, Malaysia changed its school terms from three with breaks of two weeks, three weeks, and seven weeks to four terms with one week, three weeks, one week, and five weeks break respectively. The first term runs from December 3 to February 22, a duration of 60 days. The second term runs from March 4 to May 10, . for 50 days. The third term runs from June 3 to August 2, a duration of 45 days. The last term runs from August 12 to October 25, for 55 days. November also has two and a half weeks reserved for examinations for upper grades. This schedule change was used to be more compatible with the annual monsoon flooding in the East from the China Sea.

The free and compulsory Saturday classes run from 7:30 to 9:45 a.m. for grades 4 through 6 students. The selection includes self-defense classes, red cross training, or scouting. The PTA (Parent and Teachers Association) and a private firm pay for the cost of a computer teacher. Students paying M$15 monthly can have instruction on the six computers before or after regular school hours. The PTA advisor is also the headmaster of the school. The chair is one of the board's eight parents. Seven teachers are either appointed or selected by the board. In 1989, the PTA published a one-inch thick historical book that covered fifty years of school history. It was filled with colored photos and considerable advertisement. Each class performed at the state dinner fund raiser. M$5,000 was donated by the former PTA chair.

The capital of the thirteen Malaysian states lies also on the southern tip of this peninsula. Two states are located on the island of Borneo. The two are separated by Brunei, an independent nation. The nine states that have heredi-tary rulers elect the head of state and his assistant. They then serve a term of five years and cannot be re-elected successively.

Malaysia is among the world's largest producers of rubber, tin, and palm oil. Other major products include petroleum, timber, and pepper. Malaysia, once Malaya, gained its independence from Great Britain in 1957. Like Hawaii, the national flower of Malaysia is the hibiscus.

Indonesia

February 3, 1990

The islands of Indonesia would stretch from Oregon to Bermuda. Pulau Batam is but one of these 13,677 islands. It is a 20-minute $13 ferry ride south from Singapore. It was here that I visited SD Negeri No. 015 elementary school.

At the dock immigration point, I took a taxi to the school. There I found that the children were having recess while eight of the 18 teachers were sitting at desks around the walls of the office. No one spoke English. An American/Indonesian second grade student was brought to the office and acted as our translator.

About 530 boys and girls aged 6 to 13 attended this public school. Some would attend classes from 7:30 a.m. to 12:40 p.m. while others would attend from 1:00-5:30 p.m. The different sessions also had different instructors. Students are taught math, spelling, reading, physical education, art, music, and writing in the Indonesian language. There are no telephones, computers, or television at the school. Parents do not help at the school nor do they participate in a PTA-type program.

We visited a classroom where two maroon and white uniformed sixth graders were sitting at one desk. A take-apart human torso, world globe, and textbooks were brought into the room to enhance my photography.

One of the teachers of Islam also had a car and graciously drove Eva, age 8, a male teacher and me to the four streets by four streets downtown stores located ten minutes away. After looking at vases, batik, stuffed toy animals, food, etc., and several good-byes, I finally took a cab to the Hilltop Hotel.

On the way to the hotel, the taxi picked up three secondary students going to afternoon classes. I was surprised to find one girl asking and answering questions in English.

The hotel was a very pleasant surprise. It had a beautiful view of many green triangular islands, two swimming pools that were virtually empty of swimmers, and a 30% occupancy rate at $45 per night! The two-lane roads in the area cut through thick green rain forests. Blue skies, puffy clouds, red ti plants, xoria, cup-of-gold, palms, and balmy breezes were soothing relief from the 95°F February heat.

Brunei

February 6, 1990

The *New Straits Times* January 30, 1990, stated that 21 of the top 25 Asian tycoons were Chinese. The Sultan of Brunei was the richest in Southeast Asia with personal assets in excess of $25 billion. The sultan is 46, has two wives (he is allowed four), and ten children.

Brunei is a 2-hour flight to the northeast of Singapore. It is located on the northwest coast of the island of Borneo. Two Malaysian states and the Indonesian district of Kalimantan also share this island. Brunei has no taxes for its residents and no national debt! The climate in February is quite damp with an average of 82% humidity and temperatures around 90°F. The capital, Bandar Seri Begawan, is surrounded by rolling lowlands while 70% of the land's primary and secondary tropical rain forests are in the interior.

Brunei (formerly Royal Dutch) Shell's refineries export 13% of their oil to the United States while nearly all of the liquefied natural gas is exported to Japan. The Brunei government is the nation's largest employer followed by Brunei Shell. Brunei Airlines is the third largest employer.

Printed government brochures show expenditures of 15% of the GNP for education, 24% for the armed forces, 37% for miscellaneous services, and 24% for public works. The national language is Malay while Islam is the official religion with mosques being given construction priority. A stadium has been built with four more in the planning stage. The famous gold-topped lagoon mosque was completed in 1958. Also famous are the 100-year old water villages of 1,000 wooden and concrete structures built on stilts on the river coast. Motorboats and walkways connect the communities.

Brunei became a British protectorate in 1888. During World War II, Japanese forces occupied the country for nearly four years. In 1959, the same year that Hawaii became the fiftieth state, Brunei gained its internal self government and became fully independent in 1984. This allowed for the continuation of the heredity line of Islamic sultans that rule the nation.

Malays make up the majority of the 242,000 people with about 45,000 Chinese, 18,000 indigenous peoples, and a few expatriates. Of interest is the passport validation that was in place in 1990. It read: "not permitted to go through any form of marriage with a citizen of Brunei without prior written approval from Immigration." Another interesting quirk of its culture demands that one may point only with the right thumb.

There are 293 government schools including 5 vocational-technical schools, 112 pre-school centers, 153 primary schools, 18 secondary schools, a nursing college, and a university with 912 students. The university offers courses in education, management, science, arts, and social studies. Non-governmental schools number around 69 and are either Chinese mission schools or private schools.

Headmaster Flj Mohammad Flj Tarih at Sekolah Rendah Dato Godam supervises one of the primary water schools built in 1972. This rectangular building has walkways on four sides and between its rooms. The morning session of children (250) are in kindergarten, third, fourth, and sixth grades. They use one room for physical education and recess. There are 27 teachers from Great Britain, the Philippines, and Brunei who work for about $300 monthly from either 7:15 a.m. to 12:30 p.m. or from 12:45-5:30 p.m. School terms begin in January with a forty-day holiday in March for the Islamic fasting holy days. The second term ends in August with a two-week vacation. The final term runs in December with another two-week vacation.

I was allowed to walk by the classes and photograph them from the doorway. One class was reciting English from a text. Primary classes through grade 3 use Malay as the instructional language; English begins in grade 4. Teachers move from room to room while students remain in a single classroom for the duration of the session. Islamic religious study is compulsory for Moslem children. classes are about one and a half hours per week. Transportation to and from school was either provided by parents or students would hail a water taxi from the nearby pier.

The former sultan installed electricity and water for the villagers. His picture was removed from the post offices, schools, stores, and other buildings when he gave his son, then 21, the title. The present sultan's picture with portraits of his wives placed slightly lower on the left and right of the sultan's image appear everywhere.

The International School BHD in Brunei is not affiliated with other schools that bear this name. The English headmistress is married to an Australian. There are 48 teachers (no Americans) for the 498 students. Grades K-6 are offered and classes run from 7:30 a.m. to 12:30 p.m. Special teachers are employed for lessons in French, swimming, physical education, remedial work, music, and Malay. Upon completion, students are sent elsewhere to boarding schools. The British school term system of September to August is followed.

The Brunei government's long-term goal is to have only Bruneians employed in their nation, but until the necessary skills are developed among the general population, others are asked to come to the nation for a one-year time period (usually stated in contract form). The local paper ran this ad: "Teachers wanted urgently. Interested parties please write to The Principal, P.O. Box 2098, Bandar-Seri Begawan, Brunei 1920. Preferably English Native spoken."

One final note—if you fly to Brunei on Brunei Airlines, you'll get a delicious piece of chocolate candy marked, "Hawaii."

Bangkok, Thailand
February 13, 1990

The Bangkok newspaper, *The Nation*, February 13, 1990, stated: "Tourism is one of Thailand's top foreign exchange earners. 1990 is the Year of Cultural Tourism. The trend is to entice one to stay longer and spend more. U.S. Ambassador Daniel O'Donohue and his wife are hosting a Hawaiian luau. Chefs from Hawaii's Halekulani Hotel and the Bangkok Oriental Hotel are sponsoring a nine-day Hawaiian Food Festival."

The hotels in Bangkok were so reasonable. We had two $7.00 buffets in five-star hotels! Even transportation was a bargain at 12¢ for a boat or bus ride.

Thailand has a long and fascinating history. It is not large by Western standards as 55 million people live in an area approximately the size of France. Thailand, once known as Siam, contained the world's oldest Bronze Age civilization. It flourished in the northeastern part of the country over 5600 years ago. Buddhism first appeared in Siam in 300 BC as it was introduced by Indian missionaries. Today, ninety percent of Thai citizens are Theravada

Buddhists. In 1782, the first king of the present dynasty, Rama I, established his new capital at Bangkok. This riverside village's name means to "village of wild plums." Today, King Rama IX works with a national assembly, a cabinet, and a state judiciary system.

Pearl S. Buck, Nobel prize winning author of the book, *The Good Earth*, has a foundation center in Bangkok to help Amerasian children. The staff of 65 serves over 2500 young people and their families.

I visited one of Thailand's orphanages, the Phyathai Babies' Home, and photographed some of the 300 children there. One child wanted to be picked up, so I held his hand and took a picture with my other free hand. One of the two social workers gave us a tour of this facility which was built in 1955 to house children from infants to age 5. These children have either been abandoned or have come from homes that have been torn apart by extreme poverty. The orphanage has three teachers, 70 nannies, seven nurses, three volunteers, and a doctor who visits at least once a week. There are two other homes for infants—one which sees to physical needs and another which handles infants with mental problems. Boys ranging in age from 6 to 18 are housed in one home while girls in the same age range are housed in another.

The daily routine begins with a bath for the children at 6:00 a.m. followed by breakfast, exercises, milk and snack, and classes until 11. Lunch, another bath, a two-hour nap, another snack and milk, free play in the garden on swings, dinner at 4 p.m., a third bath, television watching, and free play until 8 p.m. round out the balance of the day. The home receives about 12 new children each month. Usually more than half of them are infants.

Older children learn writing, drawing, the English alphabet, and some basic English vocabulary. About one third of this group are available for adoption. In order to pay for the cost of caring for these children, a special fund - from the National Lottery was set aside. Donations are accepted. Letters of inquiry concerning donations and other details should be addressed to Superintendent of the Home, 264/1 Rama 6 Road, Phyathai, Bangkok, Thailand 10400, telephone (66) (2) 245-5635. The Interior Ministry of Thailand's Public Welfare Department works with various Hawaii adoption programs.

Place an American college graduate in the National Library of Thailand and instant illiteracy occurs! The bulletin board displayed colorful pictures; however, I was unable to read the captions (written in Thai) and I was unable to determine what the pictures were! A collection of 16 different English primary dictionaries were to be found there. This collection included one that I particularly liked entitled, *Words to Know*, by Standard Educational Corporation, 1984. Upstairs, some of the science books were written in English as well.

I sat at one of the twenty tables with six chairs each. High school students in white shirts and blue shorts also enjoyed the air-conditioned facility—a relief from the 93°F February heat! One book that I was browsing through did not seem to have a publishing date. It did have the following phrases in English: "This Reader on Corruption(!), edited by...and...has been made possible by a grant from the Asia Foundation and the support of the Ober Foundation, New York." Turning to the center of the book, I found one page that contained only 21 lines of print; the second line of print contained 45 symbols with no spacing. The balance of the print contained spacing which may have substituted for punctuation. One word looked like it contained a backward "c" and "r," two 6's and a 9 with inked ovals. The references for this text were in English. Most of the sources ranged in date from 1920 through 1965, with the latest one being 1984 in New York, "a Plunkitt of Tammany Hall."

The five-story library contained two wings. It soon would have a (former) Soviet Union Exhibition— *Perestroika* in Action. The Soviet Foreign Minister was in Thailand to initiate an economic commission that included not only Thailand, but also Indonesia, Singapore, and Malaysia.

Cairo, Egypt
February 18, 1990

T he population of Egypt increases by 3000 people every day! Cairo is the largest Arab city in the world. Along with this burgeoning population has come an extreme housing problem that has created an area known as the "area of the living dead." Shelters and hovels have been constructed on top of the huge town cemetery. This is not supported or encouraged by the city. The area is quite unsafe. Water must be carted in. Photographs of life in the walled area are not to be taken.

Once the average Western tourist begins his or her jaunt down the streets of Cairo, one hears, "Welcome to Egypt. Are you from England or Germany? Come with me, my store is there." This will happen to you regularly when touring in Cairo. Everywhere you will be reminded that Egypt is a special country when you see nearly a third of the male population in robes and women in *el hegabs* (head scarves).

Cairo's Egyptian Museum sits across the street from the Hilton Hotel (built in 1957) on the Nile. The museum has caskets, mummies, statues, and two blue horses on display.

Taxi drivers offer personal tours of the city and the Coptic churches. A tour costs about $15. Usually tourists that are staying at the same lodging place will group together and take these drives to see other museums, 10-year-old students learning carpet weaving, and the step pyramid.

Our cab driver stopped beside a solid green fence. He knew where to push and, behold—a school appeared on the other side! The junior high school students were in gray uniforms standing at the entrance and kindly directed us to the headmistress who, unfortunately, did not speak English. Another official appeared and told the driver that the school officials might get into trouble with the Ministry of Education if they allowed us in. Thus, the school officials would not answer any questions and offered nothing in writing. regarding the curriculum.

Another day, I ventured to an elementary school that I had spotted accidentally as parents were picking up their children and were exiting from a narrow doorway near our hotel. I got to the courtyard where the principal was conversing in French with another adult. She also spoke English and informed me that no information could be given out about the school. I was not allowed to photograph the first graders' hallway drawings. While I was ushered to the street, I remembered - "Welcome to Egypt."

Around the corner from my hotel was the American University of Cairo which was established in 1919. The Fall 1988 brochure stated that AUC has the largest student body of any American university abroad. Academic classes were taught in English with a student-teacher ratio of 15:1. One third of the faculty were American while slightly more than half were Egyptian. Annual tuition cost $6800 while summer school cost $1700. The AUC was to host the 1990 Conference, "Peace and the Environment." A Mr. Kito, the chairman of one of the largest international companies in Japan, had recently donated $10,000 to the university in appreciation of the quality of education he received there.

I sat in the canteen garden of AUC and chatted with a Muslim woman from a nearby country. She was studying civil engineering to follow in her father's career. Though she was not wearing the *el hegab*, she did tell me that Muslims pray five times each day—4:30 a.m., noon, 3:30, 6:00, and 7:00 p.m. Friday is a special day with prayers held in the mosque from noon until 2:00 p.m. Women, if they attend, are required to go to a separate area. This woman's mother was a director of a Muslim international co-educational school that served nursery students through grade 9. After grade 7, the two sexes are separated into different classrooms. As a director of the school, she required female students to wear the el hegab usually starting at age 6, but she often did not wear one.

While walking around the AUC campus, I chatted with five Christian women who were participating in a two-year secretarial program. Their classroom had 20 chairs with a right-arm table for writing. Nothing was posted on the classroom walls. The universal green chalkboard was clearly in evidence. On the second floor, there was a lab that contained 12 computers. Through a window on the ground floor, I saw ten computers reserved for staff use. Red, green, and yellow chairs were in the garden. The three-story library building was closed.

The hall bulletin board contained these notices: the Political Science Association would show a movie about refugees in Africa, the Management Alumni Club would have a speaker at 6 p.m. present a talk about Energy and Business Development in 1990, the Egyptian Chamber Orchestra was giving a free concert of German music, a request was listed for blood donations, students were encouraged to express their opinions by writing for Wall magazine.

Map of West Europe

Athens, Greece
March 8, 1990

Athens, a city of three million people, contain, hundreds of famous pre-Christian statues, build ings and history. My visit to Athens would be a solo one as my traveling companion complained of leg pains which were the result of a fall into a sidewalk hole in Singapore. She decided to stay with her son in England and not continue with our trip plans. I missed her as I strolled the concrete city of Athens.

Since I would be spending some time here waiting for warmer weather (55° now), it seemed like a good idea to enroll in an intensive beginning Greek language course which began at 9 a.m. and lasted until noon. I missed the first class but I was enthusiastic about attending. One classmate who was originally from Lebanon had lived in Greece for 12 years. A Virginia woman had taken a prior course in Greek. Another woman was motivated to take the class because she had married a local man.

The class was being taught with the assumption that we had some background in the language. I made notes of the Cyrillic letters—a triangle is d (delta), a circle with a horizontal line is 'thee' (theta, pronounced as the diph-thong "th"), while a circle with a vertical line is "fee" (phi) and pronounced like "f". The character that resembles n (pi) is pronounced as "p" and the character that resembles p (rho) is pronounced as "r". The change of letters and sounds continues. I did very well in copying some of the sentences from the first lesson. When we had to recite, I would write what I had heard using English phonics and then could repeat the short phrases. When we had to use the text and sight read, I was totally lost. I had no idea what we were reading.

The majority of language teachers with whom I have visited feel that single language immersion is the best way for students to acquire another language. I don't agree and felt very grateful to the students who gave me English language explanations of our lessons during breaks. When I inquired about easier beginning courses in Greek, my instructor only laughed. During class, pictures were held up, but they could have depicted several ideas. For new vocabulary words, I would copy the Greek from the green chalkboard, but I had no idea what the words were. This introduction to Greek was enough in one session to cause me to follow the procedure to request and receive half of my $140 refund.

While visiting a Greek folk art museum in Athens, it was a joy to see third graders express pleasant surprise at what they saw—animal skin masks, shadow leather puppets on a 12' horizontal screen, silver and gold jewelry, breast plates attached to photographs, life-size models with elaborate hand-made costumes with pleats, lace, embroidery, fur, collars, and head metal-coin dangles. The wearer's age, social position, and marital status determined the pattern, style and color of a woman's dress on display.

Athens has two immigrant public schools which serve grades 1 through 6. Children of mixed marriages, refugees or Greek parentage who have been abroad can enter this school which has a teacher-student ratio of 1:15. Other public schools in Athens have a teacher-student ratio of 1:28. Classroom instruction is in Greek but English lessons are a part of the curriculum. About 300 students attend from 8:30 a.m. to 1:30 p.m. Students are taken on monthly excursions. At age 13, another language (German, French or English) is offered depending on the school location.

Private schools offer English instruction after the regular school day. Students are encouraged to spend at least three years in school but are welcome for the entire program. Apparently other teachers, parents and students do not resent the extra attention given to these students by the immigrant schools as there is a general consensus that children from the above backgrounds need this additional attention. I wonder how long the students feel the language frustration. Now I understand the expression "It's Greek to me!"

Athens is a brisk 50°F in March; it is usually windy but sunny. The breezy climate helps one to enjoy ouzo (licorice wine), cooked grape leaves, and Vienna coffee. Vehicular pollution trapped by low mountains and many heavy- smokers might make one consider visiting some of the 166 islands that surround most of Greece.

A one-day boat ride across the Aegean to Poros and Hydra was popular with Japanese college students on break (there were over 500 in a group when I went). During the cruise Greek musicians entertained us while a Yugoslavian led a Puerto Rican tourist group in a samba, I sat next to a Kailua, Hawaii, couple.

Educational tidbits taken from the March 7, 1990, edition of *Athens News*: "Walter Annenberg, former U.S. Ambassador to Britain, will contribute $50 million to the United Negro College Fund, which serves 41 black private colleges. The largest gift to a single institution was made by Robert Woodruff, former chairman of Coca Cola. He gave $105 million to Emory University in Atlanta in the late 1970s. Also, the World Bank pledged to double its lending for teaching projects in developing nations. The five-day Thailand conference had 1500 delegates. The World Bank will help countries set up policy with attention to education for girls, science, and technology programs."

Map of Italy

Rome, Italy
May 17, 1990

One month is not enough time to visit Rome! It takes time to discover its many parks, travel throughout the city to discover famous fountains, notice each building's decor, absorb the greenery between apartments. Imagine living in Rome since before Christ and then to help build its marble cathedrals and thirty-foot tall brick walls! Thirty obelisks from Egypt are here as well as innumerable Greek structures, famous sculptures, and ceiling paintings. Obelisks are a symbol of Egyptian wisdom.

The one word I would use to describe Rome would be "arches." They cover doors, windows, bridges, gates, etc. This is The City of all cities—a city full of history, art, restored architectural wonders, buildings, and beauty.

When one travels alone, sometimes miracles happen. A highlight for me was to be four feet from Pope John Paul II during his weekly 11 a.m. audience with tourists (attendance averages over 7000). It was impressive to hear him speak in several languages and see the various nations' tourists return his three-minute greetings by waving, tossing objects, or singing as did a group from Poland and a black choir from Brooklyn.

The private American Overseas School of Rome has 400 students ranging in age from pre-school to grade 12. The students represent about 40 nationalities. Roughly three-quarters of the faculty are Americans—there were no openings for elementary teachers. Italian law provides that previously employed teachers must be hired first. Maternity leave with some pay is also legal. The Canadian kindergarten teacher was reimbursed for attending an early education conference in Milan. In this kindergarten class, I met little Melissa, a girl recently arrived from the Big Island, Hawaii.

Classrooms are somewhat specialized in that students leave their homeroom for special lessons in English or Italian as well as for physical education, art and music. (The elementary librarian spent the month of December with her brother in Kailua, Hawaii.) A typical school year runs from September to mid-June. Classes begin at 9 a.m. and end at 3:20 p.m. Elementary parent-teacher conferences are held in November and April with report cards being sent home in January and June. Parents often assist in instruction by voluntarily speaking to classes in middle and high schools. The parents talk about their own skills, travels, or interests. Outside speakers are also brought in on a regular basis. Grade 3 classes spend a week in Greece. Drama students travel to London, Stratford-upon-Avon, and participate in the International Acting Festival in Vienna. In January, students participate in the International Relations course offered at Holland's model United Nations' student conference.

The six-acre campus villa is located eight miles (13 km) from downtown Rome. It includes a hillside amphitheater, two tennis courts, softball, basketball and soccer fields. At the time, Italy was preparing to defend its sixth international soccer title. The American Overseas School of Rome (AOSR) participates with the U.S. Department of Defense schools as well as with other independent American schools in Italy. The student-teacher ratio is about 12:1. Financial investment by parents runs between $5000 and $10,000 annually. Some embassies will pay one half of the tuition for their employees' children. Students' families are also connected with NATO, the United Nations, or are artists, professors on leave, or employees with overseas companies. The American Community Organization of Rome has meetings at the AOSR and plans Rome's Fourth of July celebrations.

Rome's YWCA has rooms with two or three beds in one section while another has dorm-style rooms for refugee women. My roommates were Italians that spoke no English. My pocket dictionary became the main source of our slow communication. As I would ride the bus, I would look up the words I saw in the front section of the book, and when I needed to speak, the English words were found in the back half of the book with the Italian word beside them. Often I needed to show the book to the native speakers as they were unable to understand my accent, especially in southern Italy.

At the Y, while having a typical Italian breakfast of a hard roll with jam and a hot beverage, I met a Chinese-Malaysian woman who had just got a furnished basement studio for $600 a month. I left my suitcase with her and traveled east and south with just my large purse and a light backpack.

What a luxury it was to get on and off buses and trains without any bulky suitcases! One could also check bags at the train station for $1 each item while scouting the neighborhood for lodging or jaunting to a nearby day trip. Albergo or pensiones are the budget single room places to stay in Italy. Typically they cost around $25 per night and have a hallway bathroom facility to share. One advantage of these places is that you can meet other travelers and share time together.

While I was in Italy, I read the following news excerpts: "Britain said it will not yet rejoin the UN Educational Scientific and Cultural Organization which it quit in 1985 in a dispute over alleged mismanagement and anti-Western bias." "Japanese corporations are financing educational projects to increase the number of Japanese students in colleges in Colorado, Oregon, Iowa, and Tennessee. New school creations are the International College of America in Maryland, Washington State International University and Salem-Teikyo University in West Virginia." "Well done, Ninkai Van der Zee, from the English department of the New School 6th Winner of the European Council of International Schools Silver Jubilee Essay Competition."

Still more: "American Indian boys between ages 10-19 are three times as likely to kill themselves as others the same age." "Palm Beach, Florida, is the first in the state to agree to $30,000 starting teacher pay in 1992." The International Education is a quarterly newspaper featuring job advertisements for over 140 American overseas and international schools throughout the world. TIE, P.O. Box 103, West Bridgewater, MA 02379 - $35 annually."

"Italy's estimated non-European community immigrants represent 2.5% of the total population. Immigrants were to register with the police before April 30 or face possible expulsion. About 15% of the illegal Rome immigrants have come forward to register."

One more tidbit—when it is midnight in Rome, it is noon in Hawaii.

Florence And Southern Italy

April 18, 1990

I was in a daze in a maze in Florence! Central and Southern Italy have many medieval cities where right-brain skills are sorely needed to retrack your route. Often cars lead people through the one-way lane be-tween-six-story curving buildings. Intersections have five lanes in some areas.

Spring break brings thousands of students of both high school and college age students on bus tours, even to the small, quiet towns in Italy. The hill-top city of San Gimignano, population 7000, had arrived for half-day tours to see the churches, the palace, and family towers. The Convento di Sant' Agustino allows adults to spend the night for $16. This price provides a bedroom with a view of the rolling hills and countryside of Tuscany.

Most youths prefer to stay at the 20-bunk dormitory at Youth Hostels which are open to any age group and are found around the world in tourist areas. Kazuko and I each paid $12 for sheets, towel, blanket, and access in central Florence. Kazuko and I first met while staying at the

Athens YWCA in Greece. At the YWCA, she dormed with two others while I had a single room. Kazuko was a Japanese student studying in Pennsylvania and was currently on a four-month art history and Italian language program in Rome with Temple University (Philadelphia). In the Florence hostel, I met a woman from Ohio who was spending her junior year in college studying in France but had taken a month's break to visit Italy as had two German students and two women from England.

When I visited the city of Matera located in the arch of the Italian boot, I met a Dutch journalist who spoke both English and Italian. We toured the Sassi (rock cave homes) and met a German couple. I prejudged that she was a model (she was a medical school graduate) and that he was a rock musician (he was a thin opera singer). We were guided by a very verbal 14-year old Italian boy and had English translation provided by the Dutch journalist.

Touring the eastern and southern coasts of Italy takes some adjustment. Two Australian girls mentioned to me that they felt people were staring at us, and wondered why. Long eye contact by children as well as adults does make one wonder. Young slim women wore black and were fashionably dressed in short skirts that reached to four inches about the knees. I saw very few women of other ages. Most street corners seemed to have a set of six or so men standing and talking. It was rare to see children.

Losing weight should be easy in Italy. There were no fast food shops or hotels with coffee shops in most cities. A popular corner bar is where one goes to stand and drink espresso, a very strong one-ounce cup of coffee. The only food offered there is pastry, ice cream, or a thin slice of ham and cheese on a hard roll. Other beverages were available as well. A stomach ache can result from drinking the local tap water.

I was amazed at how often an English-speaking Italian would come to my assistance! This greatly helped me enjoy an area. Michelin's tourist guide to Italy had noted so many special places to visit that I stayed longer. After all, Giuseppi Verdi said it well when he said, "You may have the universe if I may have Italy."

Overall, I spent three months touring Italy, but it still was not enough time. The art, the history, the scenery, the cathedrals, and the movement about the nation inspired poetry from me—something I had not written for nearly 15 years!

Haiku Poetry

Inspired by Rome

Rome: The Roman brick walls!
The twenty-foot length goes on;
Filled concrete arches.

Walking peaceful Rome
Observing, missing wonders
Surprises occur.

The wide buildings curve
Separated by paint hues
The splendor of Rome.

Some leaders prefer
Making decisions for all
And dwell in the past.

The trees draw my feet.
The cathedrals put me in awe
Forward and upward.

Right brain day journeys
Left brain night writes for recall
Sleep assimilates.

Religion is the
Belief Organization.
Faith is with those thoughts.

See the pace of life!
I travel to hear flowers;
Feel the steps of time.

This strange path I'm on
Presents a time of change and
Leads to special days.

Rome: parks, dogs, fashion
Trees between ocher buildings
Traffic everywhere.

City surprises!
You watch me from your windows.
I seek the flavor.

Inspired by Florence

Center of Art Life
Recognition for some men.
Postcard souvenirs.

In daytime, I'm here.
Memories travel at night.
Europe adventure.

Picture for the mind
Taken by my heart and soul.
Wonders of the World!

What you think is so
May not be what really is.
It is called—learning.

A man and his horse
Against Tuscany mountains
Topped with snow—bus ride.

Remember winter!
The sun does not mean high heat,
On and off layers.

Ho Pinocchio!
World loves: nose, puppet, story.
Where? Who? *Collodi!*

The workings of man.
Behold the Creator's Works!
And where are women?

Two gals and three guys,
Inexpensive adventure.
Camping together.

Together, single
Pros and cons to everything.
Secret: enjoy now.

Time to be, write, see
At times alone, together
Important living.

Here I Am for You.
It matters not what we do.
Spending time we two.

Inspired by San Gimignano, Italy

Afternoon sitting,
Do birds sing at two o'clock?
Countryside listening.

Down the lane they went
Never to be seen again.
Best wishes for health.

Basking in the sun
Watching, listening, thinking while
Getting warm again.

Circle of flowers
Surround the living and dead
At times I am both.

High on a hilltop
Big wigs are we, watching towns
Grow below our feet.

It's hard to be here
While planning for tomorrow.
Which takes preference?

Moments of warmth come
In spite of different tongues
From smiles, heat, light, deeds.

What does it look like?
Night of day and dawn of eve.
I'm waiting to see.

Here I go in Faith!
Holy Spirit sets the course.
I stumble through risks.

The light is going.
I sense the need to finish.
Is there tomorrow?

Souvenirs of life:
Gadgets, trash, money, babies.
Left here for others.

Blue and red outfits
Italian men of service.
Rail transportation.

Watching land go by,
War, fear, time, toil on the soil,
Faith in the future.

Sitting quietly
Allows for relaxation
And contemplation.

Inspired by Southern Italy

I never saw a
Skinny opera singer!
Do not prejudge folks.

The traveler goes
Anywhere for no reason;
The tourist sees sites.

Hello newcomer
Show and tell me what you know
Then I will move on.

City after town
What is there to see—fashion!
Clothing, shoes, jewelry, more.

Traveler's return:
I traveled this way before.
It's still new to me.

The charm of the young—
Smiles come and go with children
The heart in the eyes.

This day in the sun
Without a car or buildings
Can bring harmony.

Each experience
Unlocks part of the inner
To bring for the I.

Opportunity
Taken by choices for growth.
A lifetime of buds.

Put me in a park
Of paths, leaves, shadows, bird sounds;
Tensions disappear.

Shopper's paradise.
Buy what after purchases?
Hong Kong decision.

Today is the day
I think of you, gone from sight;
Talks, times together.

Watching night appear,
Then seeing morning light rays;
Miracle of time.

Blind faith can give hope
A reason for everything
Seek no other source.

Another day here
To discover, enjoy and
To use my senses.

I see the flower
Facing me from your railing;
Others cannot see.

Every day is new
When you travel to places
Never to return.

Put me in the dark
And I want to sleep till moved
By some basic need.

Flashes and then gone.
Dreams, people, experiences.
Mind storage recall.

Planning a journey
Brings exciting decisions;
No cost or problems.

I greet you with smiles
Everywhere I receive stares
Different cultures.

Miracles happen
When you travel by yourself.
Special events, friends.

A cross on paper
People's hope for the future
A better living. (German vote 3/90)

Attitude and strength
There's so much to see and do!
Everything runs out.

We walk by beggars.
Mother with child, aged, wounded.
Unemployable.

Worthy or servant.
When does a human being
Become a person?

I want to be outdoors.
You prefer to be inside.
How can we relate?

Nationalities.
Where but in America
Are so many perched?

When I want to rest
I need to locate the spot
For refilling cells.

Questions for the Reader

Who am I touching?
My leg, bun, and back meet yours.
Crowded vehicle.

What is there to do?
Sleep, eat, work, play, buy, learn, watch,
Talk, hear, give, live, die.

I move through this space
Holding on and letting go.
What is important?

Why do we need more?
You are out but I am in.
Then the roles reverse.

What can be given
After you have given all?
Better quality.

When do animals
Become pets or our fodder?
Who gets to decide?

What shall we gather?
What shall we save for later?
When do we use it?

Eyes open, thoughts gone.
When you look, are you seeing?
Do what with pictures?

What is the question?
Who gets to choose the answer?
When does knowledge come?

Which is easier?
The brain gets in gear when you
Take time to read, write

Is it justified
To demand payment for the
Leaders' purposes?

Do you ever think?
Questions before decisions.
More alternatives.

Can you play a game
Without winning or losing?
The majority.

War there, Skin here—Move
Sri Lankan in Italy.
Where is it better?

The inner self guides
To near and far adventures.
Go with feet or mind?

Many forms of art.
What develops the genius?
The talent breaks through.

Riding express trains;
Where will we be at seven?
A new adventure.

Where am I going?
Look what I see! I know not
What pulls me, not you.

Which way to heaven?
Do you really want to go?
Shrine, cathedral, heart.

If I have fourteen
And you have forty-seven
How much is too much?

The Adriatic Riviera

Eastern Coast Of Italy
May 25, 1990

Mango tea, North Western Ware Hawaii t-shirts, and three Caffe Hawaii bars (a blend of Hawaiian and Brazilian coffees sold here) are all a part of Rimini, Italy, a tourist haven with golden sands which stretch ten miles south of Venice.

Here one is reminded of the less-stress travel system—a system that is based on the idea of staying in one spot and taking daily side trips. A one hour bus ride north to San Marino yielded a panoramic view from a small independent and freedom-loving Italian republic that even issues its own stamps. The Vatican City in Rome is the only other independent nation which is not a part of the nineteenth century unification of Italy.

A day trip to nearby Ravenna is worthwhile, if for nothing else, to see the famous blue and gold half-inch squares in some of the oldest mosaics in the world.

Sometimes, the only way to locate schools is to listen for the sounds of children. Gates, walls, and trees keep most schools protected from the casual observer. I rang a wall buzzer at a Rimini preschool. A male custodian greeted me and introduced me to the headmistress who called in another man. The procedure for visiting a school and taking photographs in this area required that I write a letter and leave it at the school. Someone would then come to the school and read it and decide whether or not I could have permission to visit and take photographs. Unfortunately, I knew I wouldn't be in town long enough to allow this process to take place. As I exited the premises, I noticed about 40 children, aged 4 or 5, in smocks in the play area. There were also displays of the children's artwork on the hallway walls.

Locating the public library in this city of 100,000 people was not easy. I was shuffled to bookstores. After the third bookstore, I had someone write the directions in Italian. I still walked past the library twice. Finally, someone took me to the building with an arch entryway into a courtyard. Ten feet above the street was a small sign reading, *Comunale Bibliotech* (public library).

The courtyard contained various sized mosaics on three-foot rectangular stones. The glass door on the right of the entryway had a poster on it and was locked. Luckily someone came down the stairs. As I entered, I remembered that often stores, banks, and buildings lock the door on the right side.

The receptionist on the second floor directed me to the card catalog room. The catalog consisted of two-ring notebooks that were 4" x 4" x 6". A man directed me to another room which contained an English encyclopedia. Here I discovered that Dr. Marie Montessouri was the first woman in Italy to receive a medical degree. It was awarded in Rome in 1894; this was also the site of her first primary school. She was born in this eastern coastal area of Italy.

Popular in Rimini are the writings of Italo Calvino. He lived until 1985 and had won the Italian literary award of merit for his writings of fiction. I was fortunate to get an English version of one of his books entitled, *Invisible Cities*. The book features a conversation between Marco Polo and Genghis Khan and was published by Pan Books Ltd. (Picador edition), Cavaye Place, London SW 109 PG. Calvino's creative brainstorming skills inspired me to write about my own "invisible city, which follows in part: "The City of Roses. A definite requirement here is for people to take time to smell the roses. The plants are located in the intersections so that pedestrians can sniff the sweet scents as they cross the streets. Vehicle occupants dash out of their transports for a whiff while waiting for lights to change. Even the clothing is designed with sections to attach the flowers. Local newspapers state the name of rose appropriate for the day. School rooms have motorized ceiling assembly lines of roses that raise and lower automatically during lessons."

Actually, Rimini had more rosebushes than I had ever seen. One particular plant was trained to grow across three stories of one building. I saw blooms that were 6 inches across, and on one stem I saw two different colored roses.

The author of Pinocchio took his pen name from his home town—Collodi. Recently a plant maze was created there which includes bronze statues of his storybook characters. The most impressive part was the section with a bridge that leads into the model of a 12' x 36' whale's mouth. On the two mile valley walk from the bus to Collodi, a large castle-like villa stands majestically over-looking the valley. This may have been partly responsible for the inspiration of the Pinocchio story. Even in my travels I cannot answer the question: "What is the most important factor in creativity—heredity or environment?"

Einstein said, "Knowledge is experience; anything else is just information."

Bassano Del Grappa, Italy

(Northern Mountain Area)
June 2, 1990

The British School has about 70 education centers in Italy. Available to adults only, the usual process is to sign up for evening classes taught twice a week by English instructors. The term is usually for one year. At one time, it was very difficult for Americans to get jobs in Italy because of bureaucratic red tape; however, in May 1990, a new law was passed that required elementary schools to offer either German, French, or English lessons. This may make it easier for American teachers to find employment in Italy.

I was fortunate to visit a public elementary school which had about 220 students in grades 1 through 5. An English instructor gave me a guided tour of the facility. There I saw seven computers, two bookcases of library books, a small room for tutoring, a television room with about 40 video cassettes, and a double room that was used for gym activities. Lunch was brought in and served in a classroom.

What surprised me most was that the 24 teachers job share classes. Some come two mornings and three afternoons a week for a total of 24 hours. These overlap others whose schedules compliment. Students who have elected not to take Catholic religious classes are given extra art classes. One room actually had five looms in it. This was used by teachers learning the art.

The students' day begins at 8:30 a.m. Lunch is at 12:30 p.m. followed by play time in a yard until 2 p.m. Computer and language classes follow until 4:30 p.m. This is interesting since many other schools in the area end the day at 1 p.m. Also of note is that parents help to determine the time frames utilized for learning. Regular class terms run from September 15 to June 15.

Parents' only other involvement is helping with field trips. They can sometimes be quite extensive lasting an entire day from 8 a.m. to 8 p.m.

Handicapped children are enrolled with the rest of the student body with no special provisions other than accommodating their specific disabilities. Classes average a total of 14 to 25 students each. One class rose to attention the moment I entered. Uniforms are worn by students at parental request; the school does not actually require them. Report cards consist only of comments—a practice that has not changed in over 15 years.

Throughout the area there are many different schools such as technical schools, language schools, and science academies. Italy only requires students to attend public schools until they are 14.

A 14th century Italian prince was born in this area. His name was Vittorino and he has been called the "Italian prince of educators."

While in this area, I met an Eastern U.S. couple in a museum who were participating in an elder hostel program at Bologna University which is the oldest European adult education center. They felt that it was cheaper to travel with this program. Classes were taught in English, free time was given for excursions, and all meals were included. At one time, this couple had participated in a hostel program at the University of Hawaii.

Also of note is an Italian law that requires women to retire at age 55 and men at age 60.

Bolzano, Italy

(a Northern Italy border city)
June 9, 1990

G overnmental officials from everywhere in the world should be required to visit Bolzano, Italy, to see how its residents have created a lifestyle that is in beautiful harmony with their surroundings. This is one of the few perfect towns of 100,000 people surrounded by Pre Alps and the Dolomites. There are two cable cars that run to the crests of the Dolomites. An enhanced river with three walkways on each side allows quite a variety of scenes on a daily stroll. Trees and plants are labeled for the amateur naturalist in all of us.

Bolzano is also one of the seven cities in Italy that McDonald's Restaurants has chosen as a market site. The restaurant offered seven different salads along with their regular menu. (Cheeseburgers cost $3!)

An opportunity for charity presents itself at the doors of the churches in Italy where mothers with children in arms softly beg for money. What a better place could they seek than a place of worship of the Holy Madonna. Yes, Italy has a lot of poor people, but you rarely see the homeless in the streets, drug addicts peddling their wares, or people rummaging through garbage cans as you do in the United States.

After a 12-minute cable car ride, I walked up to an Alpine elementary school. The students had already gone home for the day—they left at noon. As it was 3 p.m., the only person present was a custodian. However, he was kind enough to show me the large classrooms with eight desks that seated two students each. These spacious rooms were on three different levels. A stage with four long rows of steps for seats formed the center of this octagonal building.

Later on, I visited with a blonde waitress who told me that she had learned English when she was 15. She also told me that she had a Swiss boyfriend who taught surfing in the summer in Hawaii.

Nearly every student in the Western world has studied the history of the Italian peninsula. Italy has been invaded and ruled by Etruscans, Greeks, Romans, Byzantines, Ostrogoths, Visigoths, Lombards, Franks, Arabs, and Normans. The border cities still are changing masters. At one time, they were part of Austria-Hungary. Since there is a large German-speaking population in this part of Northern Italy, most signs are written in both Italian and German. I noticed that German tourists tend to be much taller than their Greek or Italian counterparts.

Italy has taught me some interesting lessons—not the least of which is: Relax and allow for change. This really does need to be the motto for the single traveler. One of the hotels I stayed in sported the sign, "Do not get upset with anyone or anything; remember you are paying good money for this learning experience."

Sometimes I would plan to spend the night in a certain city only to find the rooms taken because of a convention. Thus, I would be forced to change plans and stay elsewhere. I would often think I was in a particular town only to find out later that day that the town I believed I was visiting was, in fact, an hour's bus ride from the train station that bore the name—Cortina, in particular, comes to mind.

After a three month stay, I left the 750-mile long boot of Italy most of which I had scanned by train or bus. If your travel time is much more limited than this, I would recommend a two week stay on the island of Sicily where each city has special artifacts dating back to the days of early Greek and Roman settlement. The island is beautiful, too, with its spectacular scenery. Of special note are the towns of Messina, Taormina, Syracuse, Ragusa, Agrigento, Milazzo, and the Lipari Islands. Italy is a special country which displays a most creative flair in shop windows and provides a warm atmosphere of fellowship.

Innsbruck, Austria
June 14, 1990

Innsbruck is clean and graffiti free! Church bells toll every 15 minutes; cloudy skies often make it difficult to tell if it's 10:00 a.m. or 4:00 p.m. In mid-June, it is daylight until about 9:30 p.m., but still jacket weather. The nearby Alps are often enshrouded by clouds.

The ambiance in Innsbruck is a delight. It's a pleasure to eat rye rolls, find mini-supermarkets, and attend the Congress building to hear an opera. The Alpine homes are five stories high, about 50' wide, white painted concrete sides with brown shutters and brown triangular roofs. Many homes are joined together to form townhouses. This historic country of Mozart and "The Sound of Music" is quite picturesque when the sun breaks through the clouds to shine on the pastel buildings and snow-covered peaks.

The city zoo is located on a mountain ledge about 1000 feet above the town. It was there that I saw my first Egyptian vulture— a curious bird with a wrinkled golden beak. All around the zoo, fathers can be seen carrying children and pushing strollers. One can take the funicular cable car down the hillside or go to about 2800 feet above the town to a small mountain village. It is possible to travel all the way to the cloud level near the summit.

A visit to a junior high school for students ages 10 to 14 led me to a director who teaches perspective drawing six hours weekly. There is no office or clerical staff at the school. The school term runs from September 10 through July 6. The government pays for country buses and for classroom texts. About 225 students attend classes Monday through Friday from 7:50 a.m. to 1:25 p.m. They also attend classes on Saturday from 7:50 to 11:30 a.m. Class days are extended on Monday and Wednesday into the afternoon from 2:00 to 5:35 p.m. Tuesday afternoons are also utilized from 2:00 to 4:40 p.m.

Subjects include music, history, physics, geography, English, Italian, German, art, mathematics, biology, physical education, typing, needlework, and workwork. Students are also required to take classes in mechanical drawing and cooking. In 1991, voluntary classes were to be offered for the third and fourth forms (ages 12 and 13) on Commodore computers.

This lively *hauptschule* had a kindergarten house beside it. There was also another middle school next to the kindergarten. Classes in these neighboring buildings were very quiet. Parents may choose which school their children attend, but class enrollments are limited.

Munich, Germany
June 20, 1990

The third largest city in Germany is a popular tourist destination. Augsburg, an hour's train ride north west is a much older city, but Munich, located in southeastern Germany, was still preferred even by 12th century rulers. Several castles are nearby that offer some fascinating tours.

Munich's subway (S-2) takes one in about thirty minutes to the site of Dachau and its memorial to the thousands of Jews killed at this Nazi concentration camp. This facility was in operation from 1933 to 1945, and was the first of its kind the Nazis used. Records show that over 200,000 prisoners plus many non-registered victims were incarcerated here. All in all, 32 camps were set up in this area. The museum at the site has listed the nationalities of its prisoners. This list includes victims from the United States and from Greece—a nation which lost nearly 85% of its Jewish population during the Holocaust.

The following information came from the handout (in English). "Political opponents, Jews, clergymen, and so-called 'undesirable elements' were to be isolated here as enemies of the National Socialist regime [Nazis]. The camp became so overcrowded that up to 1600 prisoners had to live in one barracks built for 200. Prisoners were tortured by flogging in the shower baths. An increase in diseases and epidemics occurred after 1939. Doctors carried out biochemical experiments on prisoners. Deaths also occurred from shootings with pistols and rifles, starvation, and hanging."

After that visit, every time I saw a crucifix of Christ which adorns countless intersections throughout Europe, I could only envision the hapless prisoner, wrists tied behind the back, hanging from one of these for an hour for any infraction of Dachau camp rules.

On the 10-minute bus ride to and from the train station, the seats were filled to capacity with college students. I sat next to a Japanese youth. And even though I had not been to Japan, I could not help thinking of Nagasaki and Hiroshima.

Munich was Hitler's headquarters and was heavily targeted, but Hitler's main buildings escaped the bombs. Today they comprise a music school. The city has been restored and is home to more than 1.2 million people. It is now a modern, attractive, green city with motorized objects in shop windows, Woolworths, and a subway. Munich with its rebuilt and/or restored buildings, modernization, charm, and helpful citizens makes the events of 50 years ago seem unreal, if not impossible.

Three blocks from the train station is a school center. A new five-story school building is under construction next door. The kindergarten house had to be relocated and those students are bused elsewhere during the duration of the construction.

The *Grundschule* students ages 6 to 11 are housed on two floors with older students (to age 16) on two other floors. Classes meet from 8 a.m. to 1 p.m., with a half hour break in the parking lot. Parents are requested to send nourishing snacks to school with their children and many do. Students begin English lessons at age 10. Usually there is an hour's worth of homework each day. Once each week, students take a bus to another location for swimming lessons and participation in group sports activities. A town library bus stops at the school much like the bookmobiles in the United States. Here students may check out books to read at home. No report cards are sent home, but parents are kept informed of test scores. One hour each week is set aside for parent-teacher-student conferences. A second grade teacher told me she also teaches 4th grade music two hours each week while her students have religion or needlework classes with special teachers.

Parents do not appear to be involved in classroom instruction or assistance. A Christmas program is presented by students for parents. Classrooms have wooden movable tables with metal legs. Two students sit at each table. There is a general state plan of education, but teachers are given leeway to develop their own lesson plans. I noticed that the children felt very comfortable with their instructors and were not afraid to ask for assistance with their math homework. Teachers usually keep their classes for two years. The average class size ranges from 16 to 24 pupils with 27 hours weekly spent in lessons. Video cassettes were utilized in the instruction of science and history. There were no Saturday classes.

The school had students from Turkey, Iran, Korea, and Yugoslavia. Two teachers worked with immigrants for two years before the emigré were placed in regular classes. A custodian and his wife lived at the school. A California college student told me she felt her early years of German schooling put her ahead of American students when she entered the 8th grade, but she was behind American students when it came to analyzing literature.

Oberammergau, Germany
June 22, 1990

This city is internationally famous for its presentation of a five-hour passion play of the life of Christ. This has been given every ten years with few exceptions since the year 1680. This tradition began in 1634 as the result of prayer and a promise if the remaining 80% of the town's people would be saved from bubonic plague (the Black Death) which was ravaging Europe at the time. Ironically, the townspeople were spared while nearby towns and villages continued to suffer devastating losses from the virulent disease. The passion play was originally performed before a church altar, but with the improvements in transportation and communications, the community expanded the number of performances (100 in 1980) and built outdoor seating for over 6000 spectators.

The performance involves more than a thousand of the town's citizens on stage. The play is given with German dialogue and music. Unfortunately, non-German speakers miss half of the performance because their noses are buried in the text translations. We also got nasty looks with our camera clicking since we either did not read carefully the admonition, "no camera shooting," or chose to be independent.

It is really quite hard to believe that such a production of superb and artful presentation is performed by players who are not professionals from the theater, even with the assistance from advisors from other cities. To participate in this extraordinary event, people will make arrangements to leave their jobs for the five-month duration of performances from May to September. Some of the cast are former townspeople who return from other cities just to perform in this pageant.

Tickets are always sold out well in advance of the performances. I decided to take my chances and boarded a 6:30 a.m. bus from a nearby city and waited at the ticket booth. At 7:15 a.m., I was thirtieth in line. The first person in line had camped nearby and was there at 4:30 a.m. She was the only one to get a ticket that was turned in.

I returned to the ticket booth for the afternoon performance; this time I was fifth in line. A man came by and offered two tickets at the regular full day price of $60. A German mother and her 14-year-old daughter were first in line' they were followed by twin sisters from Holland. When they hesitated to purchase the tickets, I offered to buy one. This was another miracle on my trip as there were over 20,000 counterfeit tickets sold to people who had come from as far away as Ireland and New Zealand only to learn that their tickets were invalid. Some tour groups had tickets for only part of their group members.

Oberammergau's alpine homes are famous for the religious figures and fairy tale scenes painted on the exteriors. They are easily viewed and appreciated by anyone walking in the streets. Fortunately, this art skill is passed on to a few each generation. It is certainly appreciated by many.

One morning, I followed a biker to his school. I found the secretary's name on the wall upstairs in the building. She told me to come back at 10 a.m., then 10:30, then 10:45. About 50 of the children were involved in this decade performance from 9 a.m. to 9:30 a.m. I walked with them and chatted with a teenager. Later, I talked with the school director who told me that there was no summer school in Germany because each German state has a rotating school year. As a result, vacations in the ten areas are scattered throughout the year. The Oberammergau area this particular year would have its school term from September 15 to July 25.

For the students, computer lessons begin at age 14. The Oberammergau school program is the same as the one in Munich which is about 100 miles east of Oberammergau. Children are bused in from an 8 km (5 mile) radius around Oberammergau. The elementary school (grund*schule*) across the yard from this school has about 215 students while the middle school (*hauptschule*) has around 172 students. English has been a required course since about 1975 for students in grades (called 'forms') 5 through 9. Residents do not pay a school tax. Painting, supplies, and new buildings come from the state. Everything looked to be in perfect condition. The famous art painting style found on the outsides of homes and shops is not taught in the public school.

The kindergarten house was next door. A nun allowed me to photograph students playing in a well-equipped yard that included a sandy area, plastic tubes for climbing, and swings. The woman also brought over a cute young girl from California who was performing in the passion play with her brother. She explained to me that, "I wave a palm, but somebody has to hold me because a sheep might step on me." Her father worked for a NATO defense program in the area. About 15 children from this school were participants in the passion play.

The average school day for the kindergarteners begins at 8 a.m. and runs until 12:30 p.m., except for Fridays which end at 11:30 a.m. Certain afternoons go from 2 to 4:30. The enrollment cost is $50 per month. Each class has an educator which is usually a high school or junior college student involved in teacher education, practicum experience, or practicum schooling. The educator also has an aide.

Garmisch, Germany

June 24, 1990

Can you imagine 15 white tigers moving at the command of a trainer? A Chicago banker bought them from the zoo in Washington, D.C. The zoo received the tigers from former President Eisenhower who had received them as a gift of state from India. The white-striped cats were raised and bred in Illinois and are now "leased out" on contract to the Krone Circus, Europe's oldest (1902) and largest (300 employees). These tigers had spent four months on exhibition in a casino hotel in Malaysia but now they were performing with Krone.

The tigers usually eat about three quarters of a beef each morning and they perform twice daily in the circus throughout Europe between mid-April and mid-November. The circus consists of 180 wagons and 20 pull trucks loaded with 40 horses, a swimming pool for their hippopotamus, a giraffe, four camels, five elephants, seven alligators, a boar, a goose, and a woman who performs by putting a python's or a boa constrictor's head in her mouth. The talented performers come from Morocco, Spain, Mexico, Russia, Bulgaria, Poland, and England.

Interestingly enough, three nuns are also a part of this night-traveling community that visits some 46 cities per year. One of the nuns does costuming while the other two work in the kitchen. A 60-year-old male instructor teaches the ten itinerant children who are a part of the circus. These children ranged in age from 6 to 18. The fellow teaches them in both German and English in one of the caravans. It is difficult for the circus to keep an instructor as most of them have difficulty adjusting to the grueling travel schedule.

Children who do not respect the potential danger of the animals in the circus face a punishment of staying indoors in their home van while their friends have their usual freedom around the circus.

Mrs. Krone, the current owner of the circus, is past 75, but her talented daughter, who works with 24 white Arabian horses and white-mane-and-tail palominos on stage, plans to continue organizing the three-hour extravaganza that continues to entertain and amaze its avid public following.

Garmisch is a small city in southwestern Germany of about 28,000 people. The countryside is quite scenic and many tourists come to appreciate the snow-capped mountain peaks. There is also an army base nearby.

No matter which direction one looks, the surrounding pointed mountains seemed to be within a short walking distance. The large, quiet alpine guest houses—some with orange or blue or pink walls—are also decorated with paintings of people, scenery, and windows. This makes for a delightful walk as one enjoys the work of these talented people, even in a 55°F drizzle! The upper view is well worth an extended visit just to admire the brilliant sun (when it does shine) and the blue patches of sky.

Vaduz, Liechtenstein
June 25, 1990

Liechtenstein is a tiny nation that measures 15 miles by 4 miles. It is located on the eastern shore of the Rhine River bordering Switzerland on the west. The eastern border sports tall craggy mountains and abuts Austria. The principality lands were purchased by Prince Johann Adam and officially became an independent country in 1719. There have been no armies in Liechtenstein since 1868. Special customs agreements and the utilization of the Swiss franc as the coin of the realm in the 1920s have helped the country to prosper. Mail services and bus transportation are provided by contract with the government of Switzerland. When Pope John Paul II visited in 1985, the Swiss provided the 80 local police officers with an auxiliary unit of 800 Swiss policemen to provide proper security for the pontiff.

Prince Franz Josef II was the first person to take permanent residence in the castle above the capital city of Vaduz. The prince and his wife died in 1989 after a reign of 51 years.

Liechtenstein is one of the most prosperous countries in the world. Its population is growing steadily and has doubled since 1950 to 28,000. About 37% of its workers are involved in metallurgy, chemistry, ceramics, textiles, and provision occupations. In 1950, the value of exports from Liechtenstein amounted to 15.2 million Swiss francs; in 1988, the value of exports approached 1.8 billion Swiss francs. The government is run by a 25-member parliament whose members are elected to serve a four-year term of office. The parliament works with the head of government, his deputy, three ministers, and the reigning prince. Laws can be influenced through the rights of initiative and referendum.

The capital city of Vaduz has a population of around 5000 and hosts 50 or more tour buses a day during the summer months. Most of the one-day tourists are Americans, Japanese, and Swedes. On the other hand, the numbers of overnight visitors from Germany and the Netherlands have recently broken records. Visitors are given four-page information sheets that are available in nine languages including Chinese and Slovak. A special passport validator is available in the tourist office. Non-Liechtensteiners are made up primarily of Swiss, Austrians, and Germans. Foreigners constitute about 36% of the total population.

A half-hour bus ride from Vaduz takes one up from the valley to heaven, itself, with cattle and mountain peak chair-lifts in Malbun. It is very convenient to stay in the Swiss towns of Buchs or Sargans and bus into any one of the 19 villages of Liechtenstein. It is even possible to hang glide or paraglide with rectangular parachutes near the castle hills.

Some of the buses I traveled on had fabric-cushioned seats facing the rear of the 30-seat vehicle. Dogs and bikes

were allowed on the bus. Everyone said hoe ee (hello) and
ciao (good-bye) to the driver when we entered and
departed the vehicle. I saw two adults with 14 children
(around age 8) riding bikes to school at 2 p.m. while I was
busing around the countryside.

About 5% of the school students bike to school in good
weather; 40% come by bus. Primary students range in age
from 6 to 11. After primary school, students then enter
either an *Ober* or *Real* or junior high school. Students
attend these schools until age 16. Afterward, students go
on to the high school or gymnasium until they reach age
21. Teachers pretest students in German to determine
which level of school a child will enter .

The school I visited was an immaculate building about
25 years old located in Vaduz. It had no office. The
custodians kindly directed me to one of the seven teachers
instructing about 120 primary students. Five classes were
on an excursion to a castle and a picnic. The 4th grade
instructor, whose name was Rudolf, had an Atari 520ST
computer in his classroom. He and the leader (head
teacher) were planning to have their class bicycle four
miles to the Swiss village of Buchs to the train station. After
the train ride, they were to go on a two-hour hike to a Swiss
lake. This was to be a one-day excursion that would begin
at 8 a.m. and end around 5 p.m.

This type of excursion was quite common. Sometimes
classes would go on skiing trips or visits to museums.
Later, when I was at the train station, I photographed a
class of Swiss 4th graders who were lead by a husband and
wife who team taught the same class.

German is the official language of Liechtenstein. French
is taught to school students beginning at age 10 while

English appears on the curriculum for students ages 12. The school year begins August 15 and runs almost for an entire year until July 6. Class instruction runs from 8-11:30 a.m. and 1:30-3 p.m., Monday, Thursday, and Friday. Tuesday sessions last until 3:45 p.m.

On Wednesdays, students and teachers go home early in the afternoon. Saturdays are reserved for art and music classes and sports which last from 8-9:30 a.m.

Other lessons include twice weekly classes in religion and catechism given by either a priest or nun (87% of the population is Catholic). Girls have needlework lessons throughout each year. Interestingly enough, boys are also taught needlework for two years and then are taught woodworking. Truancy is virtually nonexistent. Disciplinary procedures involve talking with the child, the class, the parents, working/writing, staying after school, or a combination of these. Time out from class activities is not considered as part of the behavior improvement procedure.

Income taxes are quite low (7%), yet the country pays for all school needs. An overhead projector and screen are located in each classroom. Chalkboards can easily be raised or lowered. The teachers' workroom-snack area has a bookbinder, a Minolta copier, a cassette player, a phonograph, and a red IBM typewriter.

Contracts with the Swiss involve busing blind students and others who need special education to schools in Liechtenstein. The principality pays all expenses of its students who go to colleges in either Austria or Switzerland since no higher learning facilities are available locally.

Homework is assigned beginning with grade 1 (usually about 10 minutes' worth). By the time students reach grade 4, the homework load has reached about 20 minutes of work. Sometimes parents are invited to participate in Saturday classes. Report cards are given twice yearly and utilize a six point rating system where 6 represents the best score and 1 the lowest score. Students are rated in the Bible, religion, history of the country, the world, and nature. Grades are also given for penmanship, art, music, physical education, handicrafts, spelling, reading, speaking, writing, grammar, mathematics, behavior, and neatness of paperwork.

Teachers often give lessons in the library which has around 1500 volumes but no staff. The school building is used in the evenings by local soccer fans, three singing groups, and 50 musicians come for two nights of instrumental music.

Liechtenstein spends about 39% of its annual budget on education. Only taxes and interest claimed a larger percentage of the budget. In 1985, the tiny country actually had a surplus of 67,000,000 SF in its treasury.

Luxembourg City, Luxembourg

June 30, 1990

The Grand Duchy of Luxembourg is a small nation surrounded by France, Germany, and Belgium. The population of 370,000 people is ruled by a hereditary duke. (The current ruler, Grand Duke Jean married a Belgian princess.) About one-third of the country is forest land. Economic interests depend upon iron, steel, and agricultural trade. Luxembourg produces its own beer, Moselle wines, liqueurs, mineral waters, and cigarettes. The city of Luxembourg has two high plateaus separated by a gorge which has a 10th-century castle fortification in it. This fortification helped the country to maintain its independence.

Three blocks from the Luxembourg train station, 400 students with a staff of 20 teachers endeavored to learn in a building that was scheduled to be torn down in 1991 since a new school building was ready for occupancy. At age 6, grade 1 students are taught German; in grade 2, French is added to the curriculum. There are special teachers assigned to teach Catholic religious classes or moral education classes.

Teachers run classes from 8 a.m.-12 noon and from 2-4 p.m. Saturday classes run from 8 a.m.-12 noon. Teachers have four hours off from the daily classes. Those over 40 are not required to teach physical education. Pre-school teachers and students need not attend the Saturday classes. After completing a tenure of ten years, teachers may switch from grades 1-3 to grades 4-6 after successfully taking relevant tests. A teacher training program is also available only 10 km (6.25 mi.) away. Teachers can sign up for special workshops such as a four-day gestalt program and substitutes are hired to cover for them.

In 1993, with the advent of the Unified States of Europe (EC), teachers and other workers hope to be able to move to another country for employment. Already, some auto license plates showed the new symbol of the EC with twelve gold stars in a circle on a blue triangle.

The school year begins September 15 and runs to July 15 with a week's vacation in November, February, and June, respectively. There is also a two-week break for the Christmas and Easter holidays.

From the street, I noticed primary art work posted on school windows. I went in and knocked on a door since there was apparently no office or staff. A pre-school teacher whose class consisted of students ages 4–6 allowed me to photograph her students. She also spoke English. As we conversed, I learned that she had taught school for three years in Israel and had been in Luxembourg teaching for seven years. After checking with the director of the school, who was teaching a class on an upper floor, I was allowed to return to my preschool teacher's class. I also noticed that teachers have their names posted beside their classroom doors.

Brigette's class of 16 children had 14 immigrants—many were from Portugal and Africa. She teaches the local dialect with picture cards and games. Her favorite activity is student motion singing while she plays a guitar. Twice weekly, she has pre-reading, mathematics, and writing activities. Every two weeks, she changes the focus of the unit studies. City schools in Luxembourg have classes for students 3 1/2 years old who will be 4 by the following January. Excursions are often made with other regular classes to the parks, puppet plays, and dance programs.

An unexpected inspector visits the classes every two months and observes instruction and responses for from 5 to 15 minutes. A special room has video and audio activities. No report cards or homework are given in the preschool. Parents were not involved in school activities. Conferences are held the first and last months of the school term. If both parents work, students are allowed to stay at school until 4:30 p.m. to do homework, and they can remain through the two-hour lunch period in the canteen. Four of the 16 preschoolers stayed for lunch. While I was visiting their class, the students drew pictures for me describing my flying trip.

Later that evening as I read a local newspaper, there was an article depicting a painting of four children and a teacher. It sold for $23 million and was painted by Picasso.

The hotel I stayed in, Paradiso, had three 8' high murals on the walls of the stair landings. As I climbed up to my third floor bedroom, I saw palm trees, an ocean, and a golden sunset.

Brugge, Belgium
July 1, 1990

Stella is a popular man's name here as Norma is in Italy. There 'Norma' is the name of a chain of mini-markets. In Belgium, 'Stella' is the name of an inexpensive local beer. I noticed here that women usually chose kriek beer that was made from cherries. Can you believe that there are 512 different choices of beer that contained 5% or more alcohol? A young local man told me that he drinks about eight beers a day and has tried about 100 different brands.

One of the local hotels offered for sale a whale painting by Maui's Robert Lyn Nelson. Another hotel had the Gideon New Testament in four languages all in one volume.

On restaurant windows, one always saw the following words: *zimmer* (German), *chambres* (French), *kamers* (Dutch), *rooms* (English). Traveling often became quite confusing as many cities also have different spellings. Town signs are also quite fascinating with such examples as: Teater Taptoe, kinderkorting, krip knap, bit burger pils, fax food, and ik slapp me fit. The architecture is really quite unusual here. There are various shades of brick buildings that look like townhouses. They are about 21' wide and have triangular facades in front.

Belgium became independent in 1830. Now its capital, Bruxelles (Brussels), is also the commercial and administrative center of the European Community (EC). There are over 5000 international EC employees. Bruxelles has long been a crossroads center of trade for the Low Countries and northern France. The EC currently had 12 members and their plans for 1992 included a single currency. The 12 countries would allow their citizens the opportunity to find employment and reside in an EC country. Other countries, including the United States, want to be involved in the EC, but memberships have been placed on hold.

Belgian schools are funded by three sources: the federal government, the city or local government, and the Catholic church. 1990 was the first year that the Belgian government was gathering information from all three sources to determine the costs involved in education. Most students go to Catholic schools. Brugge (Brugges) has free pre-schools for ages 3 to 6, elementary schools for ages 7 to 12, and technical schools for ages 13 to 18. High schools are for students ages 18 to 21, and universities for students from 18 to 27 years of age. A junior lace school is available for students ages 12 and older to learn this skill with the use of bobbins (Bruxelles uses needles). Classes are held on Wednesday afternoons. Senior citizens can come for lessons during the day or Fridays from 6 to 9 p.m. A wedding dress collar won the 1989's first year, first place gold bobbin prize. Second place went to the creator of a black lace hat.

In Brugge, the Municipal Academy for Fine Arts can be chosen by students as an alternative to traditional schooling. However, if the student's painting, sketching, and/or architectural drawings are not up to the school's high standards, they will be asked to leave after two years. The academy has about 190 students ranging in age from 12 to 18. The faculty consists of 45 teachers. Classes are in session from September through the end of June from 8:30 am to noon and from 1 to 4:30 p.m. The nearby preschool has about 55 children whose classes run on a similar time schedule. The tourist office in Brugge has a very humorous anonymous traveler's prayer which is reprinted at the end of this book.

Belgium has always been in the forefront of striving for world unity and peace. The first president of the pre-UN League of Nations was a Belgian, Paul Hymans. Belgium was a founding member in 1945 of the UN. The first president of the United Nations Assembly was a Belgian, Paul-Henri Spaak.

Tourcoing, France
July 10, 1990

"I think I'll go to France for the day." And so I did—from Ghent, Belgium, it is only a 40-minute train ride south to this border town of about 100,000 with few tourists. Tourcoing was a textile center at one time, but most of that business had been transferred to Portugal. About 17% of the local population come from Algeria, Tunisia, Morocco, Italy, and Portugal. Foreigners were allowed to stay in the area for three months; however, if they had found no employment by that time, they were supposed to return to their homeland.

The only school for bellringers in France was opened in this town in 1971. The Royal Elementary School in Honolulu also has a group of bellringers.

Regular school terms begin September 10 and run until July 10. Public schools have about 5000 students ages from 6 to 11. There are about 3600 students enrolled in private schools. Classes run from 8:30-11:30 a.m. and 1:30-4:30 p.m. Saturday classes last from 8:30-11:30. Teachers and students are given Wednesday afternoons off.

Parents sometimes come to Saturday classes to read to students. Some parents paid extra money for their children to remain at school until 5:30 p.m., or to attend nursery school for those between 2 months and 21/2 years. A free preschool has been available for the past quarter century for children ages 2-1/2 to 6 years old.

Factories and social services organize and pay for their employees' children to attend three weeks of summer camp. The children are grouped together by ages—6-11 years, 12-15 years, and 16-18 years. The town also organizes student resident camps at a cost of about $200 for a three-week stay. The charge to nonresidents is $400. Leaders of these camps spend about 36 days in training. I saw four leaders with a group of thirty elementary students quietly sitting on red-cushioned benches in the beautiful town hall playing a competitive team environmental game.

Across the street, I treated myself to a window shopping expedition in a large, modern, air-conditioned market. I saw 13 bowls of various types of salads; English music was playing. Jogging outfits for two-year-olds were displayed bearing the words, "US Navy," while men's sweatshirts bore the logo "The American League—The First Series" and a stitching of a baseball player at bat.

I exchanged Belgian francs for French francs at the train station. It is always a good idea to have at least $20 worth of local currency when you arrive just in case the exchange desk is closed or not located at the train station. Coins for use in locker rentals, if available, and toilet charges may be obtained by buying small items such as gum, etc. In Tourcoing, I needed to see the Chief of Services to get a lavatory key.

The local bus ride cost about $1.20. (It was only 23¢ in Ghent.) Inside the bus, there was a 12 inch by 12 foot padded board that ran down the length of the vehicle for people to sit on or place packages on. While in Tourcoing, I noticed that the bakeries, as they did in Italy, wrapped their items in a special paper and sealed it with colorful stickers or ribbons.

On overseas trips, having and using two plastic credit cards can be a great convenience. I use traveler's cheques for emergencies and then replace them when I run low by utilizing a credit card. Most European banks have male tellers and getting approval for withdrawing money can take anywhere from ten minutes to three hours depending on telephone connections as there is usually only one number that a teller can use to get an approval and that number is often busy. Meanwhile, the teller must return to his window to serve other customers.

It is important to get the value of coins and bills straight when changing nations. I received 47 French francs for 300 Belgian francs or $9. I found that figuring values was much easier if I simply rounded numbers upward, i.e., approximately 50 FF = $10; thus 1 FF = 20¢. Immediately figure the value of ten units, 100 units, and 500 units of the local currency so that when you are window shopping, you will have a fairly accurate idea of the actual cost of a purchase. It is a good idea to write this information down and keep it handy as it is easy to forget these values after you have had to change them several times. Hopefully, the EC plan to have a unified currency by 1993 will be successful.

It is a challenge to visit another country. Reading about role models can make a difference. The Herald Tribune

July 5, 1990, noted that "Marion Rice Hart at age 83 made her last of seven solo sailing trips across the Atlantic." Many Europeans do make the short journey to their bordering neighbors; however, there are many Europeans who do not.

Ghent, Belgium
July 12, 1990

Ghent is a memorable city of canals, bay windows, steep sloping roofs, old four-story brick townhouses with 21 feet of interesting facades facing the street, creative doorknobs, various iron grill designs, and lace-patterned curtains. Costumed musicians from Peru were selling their cassette tapes on the streets. The population of 230,000 was geared for a week's musical festivities.

A Catholic school and city technical school are across the street from each other. At the city technical school, students aged 13-18 can study home economics or science. Professional training is given in skin and hair care, hospital aide work, and clothing manufacture. Diplomas are offered in each field. The purchase of books and supplies are the only student expenses for the 30 men and 1000 women who attend (60 students were from Turkey). The school term begins in September and continues into June. Classes start at 8:20 a.m. and end at 4:30 p.m. with Wednesday afternoons free for both students and teachers. The technical institute also offers night classes in sewing, shop window art, and English which is a two-year program. There are 160 teachers with an office staff of about 30.

The Catholic *Nieuwen-Bosch Humaniora* has 110 teachers, an office staff of 13, and about 830 students. In 1989, a new *moderne* curriculum was introduced which eliminated Latin and Greek lessons, increased the number of math courses, and introduced drawing classes. Class schedules at this school are similar to those at the city technical school. The first language offered after Flemish at this school is French, followed by English, and then German. The number of lessons required depends upon the core area chosen.

The core areas include mathematics, sciences, and economics. Each core area class offers two computer lessons weekly during the second year of the three-year program. The number of lessons required each week is indicated by a number following the subject name.

First year studies include, Religions (2), Dutch (5), French (4), English (4), German (1), the Economics core requires (3), History (2), Math (7), the Sciences core requires (5), Economics core requires (3), Economics (for core only, (4)), Biology and Chemistry (1), Sciences core requires (5), Natural Sciences (2), Geology (1), Gym (2).

I chatted with two women and their 18 students at an intersection and then followed them to their city summer school.

Once at the school, I noticed that upstairs other women were watching about 30 children ages 1-1/2 to 3 years. The children were napping and would be awakened at 3 p.m. Single parents pay $2 per day and two working parents pay $15 for these services. Care for older children ages 3 to 6 cost $5 per day. These young caretakers each have three years of schooling in child care. They work eight-hour days (teachers work six-and-a-half hour days) and must decide on their career path by the time they have reached 15 years of age. There were two other women working in the kitchen.

We walked down the street to *Institut Laurent,* identified by a black stone sign on the third floor of an unlikely looking elementary school building. Nude children slid down a slide into a plastic wading pool for happy splashing in the concrete courtyard. The institute offers supervision of children from 7 a.m. to 6 p.m. for either 3 week or 6-week sessions. Because of daylight savings time, it is light here until 10 p.m.

Of special interest is the fact that Ghent has a world-class chess club which started here in 1900. Currently it numbers 25 children ages from 8 to 12 in its membership who meet every two weeks. I visited with two brothers, - 12 and 15, who play three games daily and are anxious to get into the club.

A revamped monastery is the site for a five-day chess tournament of nine rounds. The 13th Open International Chess Festival has 381 entrants of which 13 were women. They play according to the Swiss system which is governed by the 1989 FIDE Laws for Rapid Chess. Twenty-one countries were represented including two players from America.

This is the fourth year for the July chess contest to include players to age 21. Last year's winner was an 18-year-old Israeli lad. Of the ten top players, the youngest is Florin Pantelimon, the national champion of Romania.

He is 13. He speaks French, English, and Romanian, has no siblings, has had two years of computer training, lessons with two chess trainers, and practices chess at home on a Sinclair computer. His father, a petro-engineer, taught the boy chess at age 3.

Mihai Panait, the boy's trainer, learned how to play chess when he was 6. He was taught by his 9-year-old sister. During the past three years, while giving lessons, Mihai has worked as an electrical engineer and journalist.

Although chess is enormously popular in this country, there were many other things I noticed as well. One thing that struck me as interesting was the fact that Ghent's large factories close down for vacations in July while neighboring Bruxelles (Brussels) close down for vacations in August.

I noticed a t-shirt which said "No time to waste." I spoke to a woman wearing the words, "Le Waikiki," on her sleeve. She asked me where this famous beach was located. Imagine her surprise not only to be told where it was but to also meet someone from that area.

In a moment of relaxation, I watched a peppy, bow-legged, 2-year-old in one of Ghent's city parks. Ducks, bikeways, knolls, various large trees, and walks under a waterfall make this town one of the favorite Belgian cities for tourists.

Amsterdam, Netherlands
July 22, 1990

How does it feel to be in Holland and realize that the land you are standing on is below the level of the nearby North Sea? As you ride a bus, on one side, you notice only calm water blocked by man-made wooden and concrete barriers. On the other side of the road, there is a drop of about eight yards where cattle roam on flat land (and produce 15 liters of milk daily). Does it help to know that one quarter of the Netherlands is below sea level and the last major flooding occurred in the 1960s?

Today, the waterflow is controlled by machinery. Windmills formerly pumped water into the canals leading to the sea. Mills have performed this task continuously since 1414. Working windmills are used for grinding grain and have dwindled in number from more than 10,000 to less than 200 with the advent of oil and steam driven pumps. The gradual rise from below to above sea level is virtually unnoticeable and it is easy to forget to worry about the dikes and storms on a sunny day. Holland is reclaiming land from the North Sea continuously by building a dike to hold sea water out and then pumping the water out of the diked areas.

The Netherlands is made up of 12 provinces, only two of which comprise the area known as Holland (which means 'marshy scrub land'). The Dutch language is used here as well as in the Netherlands Antilles in the Caribbean near Venezuela. Dutch is also spoken in Indonesia which was once known as the Dutch East Indies, but became independent in 1946. The queen of the Netherlands is Queen Beatrice, the daughter of the past queen, Wilhelmina. A street in Honolulu, Hawaii, was named for the former queen. The queen's husband retains the title of "Prince of Netherlands."

In the Netherlands, nearly all children between the ages of 4 and 6 attend optional pre-schools. At age 12, students may choose vocational training programs, a general course of study (chosen by the majority), or university preparation via atheneum (language, sciences), lyceum, or gymnasium (the latter two stress Greek and Latin). This nation has one of the highest literacy rates in Europe.

Students wanting to leave school at age 16 are still required to attend classes part-time for two years. About 70% of the nation's students attend private schools which are, ironically, financed by the government. Besides basic schooling (Basis school), there is *Freinetschool* (alternative education), *Kleuterschool* for ages 3 to 6, and *Rijschool* for vehicle operation lessons.

Amsterdam was a whirlwind of cheese samples, a demonstration of carving wooden shoes for fishermen or farmers from poplar or willow trunk boles, slicing the face of a diamond many times, canal rides, climbing nine-inch deep spiral steps, visiting the Van Gogh and other muse-ums. This was all part of a too-short-a-time visit to this famous tulip area. Locals and tourists alike carried long-stem colorful bouquets that were purchased for $3 from the summertime Saturday flower markets. Although many of the flowers here carry no fragrance, I know of no one that has not enjoyed their quiet beauty.

Utrecht, Netherlands
July 24, 1990

When one gets off the train in Utrecht in order to make connections to other trains going to other countries, one can become quite confused as the station houses a large, two-level shopping center. Fortunately there are banks here that provide the fairest currency exchange rates. When budgeting for Utrecht, I recommend that you allow US$50 times the number of days you plan to stay in town.

The city's public library had some rather interesting English texts: *The Great Soviet Encyclopedia* 1975, *The Grolier Encyclopedia* 1977, and the *Blue Guide Holland* book, 1986.

It is also possible to go into a Hong Kong restaurant here to order *Varkensvlees in reepjes met broccoli, boon oven azyn sesamolie* which means *Hap Tsun Yuk Pin* (!) and it only costs $9. I had not had broccoli for six months— that was the only word I needed to recognize. When my plate arrived it contained not only the longed-for broccoli but was also adorned with a rose that had been carved out of an onion and dipped into an orange dye. I also learned that I was a *niet roker* (non-smoker).

Electric rail slow trams run down the center of main streets in the city. Behind the driver there is a 7-second silent slide advertising program. Twelve slides run in sequence and then are reversed. I also noticed that soft drugs could be purchased in some public shops. Unfortunately the environment has graffiti appearing on rooftops, home walls, sides of trucks, etc.

The school that I visited in Utrecht was located beside a four-story brick water tower. It was a pre-school for children ages 2 to 4 and has about 30 students. One teacher performs most of the instructional duties which entails about 25 hours weekly including student sessions from 9 a.m. until noon. By advertising in newspapers and word-of-mouth, she was able to get eight volunteer helpers who signed a contract to work on certain days.

The school term runs from September 3 to July 21 with one week breaks occurring in October, December, February, April, May, June, and six weeks in the summer. At the time I visited, there were fifteen children on a waiting list to attend school. Other schools in the area are open from 7 a.m. to 6 p.m.

Techno Time is a company that works with Utrecht's unemployed. Employers pay the company which pays the employees' salaries plus providing health services. Techno Time has 12 offices in Netherlands and two in Belgium. Most of the jobs offered are for those with electronic skills, engineering, and building technicians between the ages of 18 and 30. This particular branch of the company began in 1984 and places about 40 people a month. Only about 2 in 480 are women.

Nearby is the Historic Costume Museum. The director of this museum started the collection when he was 18. He was motivated by a female instructor who brought costumes to an Academy of Arts class. Exhibits are rearranged here each year around a new theme. Textile students have been visiting the museum regularly since its 1975 opening date. Careful thought is given to the amount of light, its direction, the air quality, and protection for the displays. Costumed doll postcards are just one of many unusual souvenirs one can purchase here.

Utrecht is a city full of bicyclers who share some of the sidewalks and special areas of the highways. Fortunately these bikers are careful of absentminded pedestrians. Healthy people of all ages can be seen riding their two-wheelers beside cars and canals.

Copenhagen and Frederickshavn, Denmark

August 4, 1990

Private is the word to look for on signs in Denmark to locate a $25 room. I stayed in a three-bedroom apartment, 50 steps above the street.

My busy landlady was among the first women in Denmark to enter and complete a four year study course in carpentry. This was accomplished in 1976. In 1983, Helle Bergstedt completed training to become an architect. She was the only woman for about two years to lead unemployed workers in the restoration of homes. Some of her other activities involved having 250 people work with her in the staging of activities in a children's theatre.

Most of Denmark is above sea level. It consists of 483 islands of which about 100 are inhabited. Denmark also lays claim to the largest island in the world, Greenland, which had been a colony since 1380. In 1953, it was formally made a part of Denmark.

Today, Denmark is ruled by Queen Margrethe II who was born in 1940. She is the youngest queen of the oldest kingdom in Europe.

Kobenhavn (Copenhagen—which means merchants' harbor) is the capital of Denmark and boasts 15 million people. Tivoli Amusement Park and Gardens, across from the main train station, has a youth guard band which performs four times weekly during warm weather. Students ages 10 to 17 must be able to play two instruments in order to be accepted into the band. Learning begins in the first grade with five music lessons a week which include instrument playing. This marching band has been playing for over 100 years—ever since Tivoli Park opened.

While riding a city bus I chatted with a young student (14 years old) from Chicago. He and thousands of other students who play soccer were in Copenhagen to play in two tournaments. Students, parents, and coaches slept in schoolrooms which were used as hostels. Incidentally, the Brazilian team would eventually win the championship.

A famous ballet trainee lived here, once upon a time, who wrote 156 fairy tales. Hans Christian Andersen's statue is located in the spacious city hall with other famous men of Danish history.

I traveled on the train out of Copenhagen. After a while, the train was driven onto a ferry for a 45-minute crossing to another island. Then the train proceeded across the island, over a bridge, then northeast to Frederickshavn. This journey wound up covering most of Denmark in about seven hours. It was on this journey that I met Liselotte Smeo.

Liselotte Smeo assists with ticket sales for $40 ship rides through the Oslo, Norway, fjords. She attended a basic school grades 1-4, where classes ran from 8 a.m. to 1 p.m. She went on to grades 5-10 where classes ran from 8 a.m.

to 3 p.m. After the 10th grade students can choose a three-year program in a technical, business, or, as Liselotte did, the Gymnasium School with emphasis on languages. These classes lasted from 8 a.m. to 2 p.m. The school term runs from August 6 to June 21.

Danish children have five lessons a week in English beginning in grade 5. In grade ten, that number doubles, and in the Gymnasium School, the number rises to 15. She also had five German lessons weekly beginning in grade 7. In grade 8, French lessons five times weekly were added. Liselotte then spent a year in California as a mother's helper.

After that, she spent six months traveling alone around the United States. She even had been to the islands of Oahu and Maui in Hawaii for three weeks. These travels occurred when Liselotte was in her early twenties.

The city's new city hall complex includes a library, four indoor swimming pool areas, and a cafeteria for the population of 45,000 people. Nearby in a badminton gymnasium, I saw costumed folk dancers from Norway, Sweden, Denmark, and Finland. The youngest dancer was 14. Between performances, I noticed a man in an aloha shirt was allowed to dance on stage.

While I visited Frederickshavn, I was sickened to read very alarming newspaper stories:

"The majority of child pornography films were made in America, but now they are also being made in Scotland where the torture, sexual abuse, and deaths of young children are on the increase. In America, the FBI went undercover to a $10,000 fee meeting to view and buy a movie. Child pornography became widely available in the 1970s when Denmark legalized its production. Scotland Yard has a list of 3000 names of known paedophiles and associates.

"Substantial numbers of homeless children are lost to the school system and receive no formal education. At least 164,000 children were estimated to be homeless in 1989 in England. The new national curriculum could help provide greater continuity for transient children. For primary age children, poor reading, writing, and oral skills were exacerbated by poor self image and low expectations. Pupils also suffered the problems of bad diet and living in cramped conditions. Lack of sleep from sharing overcrowded rooms left children unable to concentrate.

"A Jamaican infant school teacher is one of many foreign women sentenced to seven years in England jails for transporting drugs. Many women have been hired as couriers for delivering common products like shoes, but were not told of the hidden drugs."

On a more positive note—the Newberry Book Award for the best child's story was given to Lowry for *Number the Stars* which tells how the Danes risked their lives to transport Jews to Sweden during World War II.

Temperatures in Denmark in August can reach 85°F in the day and dip to 65°F at night. The shades of blue in the water and sky are known for their special qualities. The space between cities allows for the enjoyment of groves of trees, slight hills, and bicycling for all ages. An architectural feature that I'll remember in particular is the use of angles in buildings. One hotel room had seven walls, another had five. Triangles, rectangles, and curves are often brought together in the same structure. Another surprising find was a blend of fruit and nuts called, "Kim's Hawaii Mix."

Oslo, Norway
August 9, 1990

The Oslo Chapter of Greenpeace Norway began in 1988 and now has eight full-time staff personnel with some 2000 members. Since Greenpeace is concerned with environmental issues, they have divided the areas they believe need the most attention into four sections — toxic (wastes), the atmosphere, the ocean, and nuclear (energy, power plants, etc.). The United States branch contains the most members of this active organization which is second in size only to the International Red Cross. Greenpeace has chapters in 25 countries with over four million involved citizens.

Greenpeace was founded by a group of Canadians in 1971 in protest against atomic testing. Today, seven Greenpeace ships patrol the seas. The primary ship is the *Pacific Rainbow Warrior.* The first ship bearing that name was sunk in a New Zealand harbor by the French in 1985. Interestingly, there is an American Indian legend that says that when the Earth gets sick, the rainbow warrior will come to its aid.

What a treat it was for this peace activist to visit the Alfred Nobel Institute! In Nobel's will of 1895, he requested that Sweden distribute cash awards in the areas of chemistry, medicine, physics, and literature while Norway would distribute cash awards for the areas promoting disarmament and world peace.

Relevant to this is the fact that Norway and Sweden were united in 1814 and did not separate until 1905. (The separation was a peaceful one.) In 1880, Norway took a stand in favor of international arbitration—this might have been the reason that Nobel chose Norway as the site for the awarding of this peace prize. A committee appointed each year by the Norwegian parliament has chosen the winners since 1901 when the first awards went to the founder of the International Red Cross, Mr. Dunant from Switzerland, and to the founder of the French Peace Society, Mr. Passy from France.

Austrian Bertha Von Suttner was the first woman to win this award (1905). Part of her acceptance speech included a comment about, "The instinct of self-preservation in human society...is rebelling against the constantly refined methods of annihilation and against the destruction of humanity." She is known as the inspiration for the Nobel Peace Prize and as the first woman political journalist. She wrote the book, *Lay Down Your Arms.*

Jane Addams was the first American woman to win the Nobel Peace Prize (1931). Emily Balch in her 1946 acceptance speech spoke on "Towards Human Unity or Beyond Nationalism." Both were leaders of the Women's International League for Peace and Freedom, and gave most of their prize money to this still active peace group.

The Nobel Institute Library contains many peace brochures from many different nations. The Peace Union of

Finland's flyer states, "Politicians and the military have regarded a limited nuclear war [as] impossible. Largely owing to the physical movement against nuclear war and the peace movement, practically no one believes in survival after an unlimited nuclear war—in or out of shelters."

As I browsed through the library, I skimmed through several booklets in English. I discovered a *Journal of World History*, vol. I, no. 1, Spring 1990 and found that it was published by the University of Hawaii Press. It is, indeed, a small world.

Norway is one of the most scenic countries in the world with its famous fjords, glaciers, the city of Dombas' 45-minute train ride that views 35 incredibly high waterfalls, and pointed mountain peaks. Does this environment motivate its citizens to be so concerned about the future?

Mrs. Gro Brundtland, a former prime minister of Norway, mother of four, physician, and political representative in Oslo, was commissioned by the United Nations to prepare a report on the state of the Earth. This publication which appeared three years ago was entitled, *Our Common Future*. It is used throughout the world today as a primary reference. In this report, she stated that more money went into packaging goods in 1986 than every American farmer had made on their total annual food production. When she was asked about contributions that could be made by the schools, she stated, "Children should be encouraged to think environmentally. Knowledge generates confidence. Environmental studies might well be integrated into most general subjects."

My own adventure in Norway continued on a bus ride I took to see another famous set of waterfalls. On that ride were several nine-year-old girls returning from a week of camping. There were 22 girls with four leaders sharing rooms at the tourist motel. As I visited with them, I learned that riding on the back of a goat at a cheese factory was Trudy's favorite first-time camper memory. Irene liked the two people paddling a canoe activity.

Many summer programs are organized for student groups to stay at Norway's Youth Hostels which are rated from one to three stars based on the quality of accommodations. The three-star accommodations only cost $20 and included a delicious breakfast buffet. Four women and I shared a motel type room with bunk beds and our own lavatory. These women were from Australia, Denmark, Germany, and Sweden. Unfortunately giggling youths and a snorer kept me awake in this modern lodge that faced a lake. Early the next morning while I stared out the window, a low white cloud split the nearby mountain horizontally. The beauty of this nation is unforgettable.

Northern Norway

August 18, 1990

I t is said that in Norway, many people go through Hell. Some stop and become part of the 100 residents. I only spent three hours in Hell and am very happy to report that I recognized no one. The temperature in Hell, Norway, (population 100) in August at 5 p.m. was only 75°F and nothing was on fire. The easiest way to get in and out is via Norway's quiet, clean, large windowed trains. Many people arrive at the neighboring town by plane. The main hotel nearby will charge $100 a night for a single, if you remember to ask for the summer rate. Hiking about a mile from the village will reveal two very old stone carvings of reindeer with vertical lines under the neck. By the way, *hell* in Norwegian means "luck." I was the only one to leave Hell on the train that continued north along a calm, majestic fjord.

On the train, I met a 13-year-old blond boy, Egil, who was taking the three-hour ride home by himself after visiting his grandmother. The boy's father works for a steel distribution company. His mother was a schoolteacher and had taught her son in grades 1 through 3.

According to my new friend, the school term in Norway runs from August 22 to the middle of June. Egil would be entering seventh grade in a school with 26 students. There were only eight students in his sixth grade class.

Elementary classes in Norway are quite small in number of students, ranging from six to nine per grade; often, teachers have combined classes. Teachers are also responsible for obtaining library books on loan from the local libraries. At age ten, students are introduced to English, and at age 14, they are introduced to German.

Egil's class day began at 7:30 a.m. when he caught the bus. Classes began at 8:30 a.m. and ran until 2 p.m. Most students would bring their lunch, but food could be purchased at the school's canteen. Part of Egil's day included two hours of homework. His sixth grade class had a 1980 model Tiki computer (made in Norway) with a printer which was used to write English and practice reading skills. Every other week, his class would take a bus to an indoor swimming pool about 14 km (8.7 mi) away. March excursions would include skiing, track, and snow survival lessons.

The elementary school that Egil attended had two male teachers and seven female teachers. Three teachers worked with the kindergarteners ages 3 to 6. Grade four students were taught knitting, sewing, and woodworking, regardless of gender.

Egil liked the winter season best because scooters could be used in the mountain snows. He wore a jogging outfit that had printed on the top, "Kick off in Play, USA."

The many gray days of winter led the Norwegian parliament to pass a law requiring automobiles to be driven with their lights on both day and night. There are statistics that conclude that this results in fewer accidents. Colorado is the only American state to have such a requirement.

My next destination, Bodo (pronounced, "Buddha"), is above the Arctic Circle. The Gulf Stream keeps the water unfrozen in winter and offers 60°F weather in August. The two-year-old Bodo airport continues the Scandinavian flair for combining curves and angles in the construction of its buildings. This results in a feeling of freedom from the routine four walls. Incidentally, my lunch of reindeer patty, carrots, broccoli, and baked potato came with two slices of green mango.

If one makes it this far north, a boat should be taken from Bodo to the very special Lofoten Islands to the northwest. These beautiful islands are surrounded by jagged mountains and are worth several days of leisurely touring. This area gave me the feeling of Windward Oahu but with far fewer cars and people. About 30% of Norway's residents live on some 600 islands.

I would like to visit these islands around the summer solstice in order to experience the midnight sun.

Central Finland

August 21, 1990

At various times, Finland has been a part of the Swedish Empire and the Russian Empire- Thus, Stockholm and St. Petersburg were both former capitals of Finland- Through several treaties, Sweden gave about one-sixth of Finland to Russia in 1807. In 1884, the equal status of Finnish and Swedish languages was legitimized. In 1906, Finland became the second country to permit women to vote. New Zealand was the first in 1893 while the first American territory to allow women's suffrage was Wyoming in 1893. After the Russian Revolution in 1917, Finland gained its independence. Following World War II, Finland lost about a tenth of its southeastern section to the Soviet Union. The Finns were able to remain neutral and work with the European Economic Council (EC) and with Soviet Russia prior to the collapse of communism. COMECON, the United Nation's peace-keeping forces won the 1988 Nobel Peace Prize. Finland has more men in the U.N. forces than any other nation except for the United States.

Autumn begins in mid-August here. Tourists are already gone, even though the weather is a sunny 60°F. I liked the town of Oulu, population 100,000, with a city council of 59 representatives. To me, the word Oulu seemed like a combination of the words Oahu and Honolulu. The university which was founded in 1958 has a teaching staff of 920 including 80 who are involved in teacher training. In 1989, the student enrollment was around 900.

The campus' geological museum has one of the best exhibits of rocks I had ever seen. (The very best exhibit was in Singapore on Sentosa Island where rocks and gems from China had been taken to Taiwan and later displayed in this famous clean-green city.) I noticed in the Oulu museum that there were two rocks labeled, "Havaiji, USA." One brown stone was labeled, trakyytli, while another rock with a black hole in it was labeled, alkaliolivianibassa-Otti. A pahoehoe lava rock was displayed that had been found in Iceland.

The campus buildings were connected by wide, windowed hallways. The two-year old, curved and angular library had over 1.2 million volumes. The latest English language book I found was the McGraw Hall Encyclopedia of Science and Technology (1960). Of interest was the book, Oecologia, which was printed on acid-free paper. In this book, the editor of the flora (plants) section from the University of St. Louis and the editor of the fauna (animals) section from the University of North Carolina had worked with two editors from Germany in cooperation with the International Association for Ecology (Intecol). Three volumes of information from the World Education Encyclopedia by George Kurian (1988), Facts on File Publisher, New York, provided details about the Finnish educational system. Material was also drawn from the reference,

Lifelong Education for Adults, an International Handbook, by Colin Titmus, Pergamon Press, New York (1989).

Do modern universities make the educated person? Winston Churchill wrote, "The empires of the future are the empires of the mind." My question is, "Are our minds, attitudes, and actions being controlled by what we see on television and read in the newspapers?"

In Kuopio, Finland, some day care centers take year-old infants. In one particular center, I observed three adults caring for l2 toddlers in a remodeled house. Across the yard were 20 children age 4-6 with two teachers and an aide who worked with the children from 6:30 a.m. to 5 p.m.

Finnish schools operate from mid-August to the end of May. This term is also the same for preschoolers. Elementary students go home at different times between noon and 2 p.m. Lower grade teachers usually teach older students for an hour after the younger students have gone home. Students begin their lessons in Finnish. At age 9, their parents may choose a course of study for the students in either English or Swedish. At ages 13-16, the students in the comprehensive schools are taught in either Swedish or Finnish. Both languages are official (since 1902) even though only 8% of the total population of Finland is of Swedish stock. However, since Finland was a part of Sweden for nearly 500 years, this is not surprising. Throughout Finland signs are labeled first in Finnish and second in Swedish.

Tampere, the second largest city in Finland (population 175,000), can boast that in 1882 their weaving factory was the first company in northern Europe to install electric lights. Today, Tampere's public library is open even on Sundays where I saw many local citizens reading.

For the past 11 years, a local bank in Oulu has sponsored an annual youth competition in running, shotput, and the long jump. About 400 boys and girls between the ages of 6 and 12 try their best in this event. They usually wear hot pink and purple outfits and stand out brilliantly against the background. When the events begin, a starter fires a gun into the air and yells something that sounds like, "follow me," but the starter does not move.

While I was writing my notes about Finland and eating an oval pizza with blue cheese, ham, and two slices of pineapple, I heard the taped music of *Aloha Oe*. In Finland it was called *Aloha A*. Part of the song was in English, but the rest of the song was not in any recognizable Hawaiian that I had ever heard. Also, the pizza here is definitely Italian style. It has a crust so thin that one eats it with a knife and fork.

While I was in Finland, I noticed beaded car seats, automatic doors, escalators that moved when a person came near them, Kiwi fruit from Italy, free medical care, $7 open-faced sandwiches on a single slice of bread, and $2 bus rides. This land of 187,000 lakes is a special, modern nation.

Southern Finland
August 31, 1990

Since May 1990, a new English-language newspaper, *The European*, has appeared. A donated page to the World Wide Fund for Nature mentions that four out of five children with leukemia survive thanks to the ingredients found in the rosy periwinkle, and, on the same page, man is destroying rain forests the size of Austria every year. I saw this paper while I was visiting Finland.

Traveling around the world stimulates an interest in a magazine called *Current History* which is published in Philadelphia, Pennsylvania. It gives a monthly review of special events by country.

The city of Turko (Turku), Finland, on the southwestern coast is the oldest city in the nation. It houses a harbor where eight summer ships travel to and from Sweden during warm weather. It is a beautiful eight-hour journey that takes one past many tree-covered islands.

In Turko, I visited a gymnasium school that has 220 students ages 16 to 19. The general school across the street has about 380 students ages 13 to 15. There

Christianity is taught one hour each week. In the gymnasium school, the same course is taught two hours each week. In this city of about 150,000 people, there are nine of these gymnasium schools. Some are known for their instruction in music, some in art, and others in science.

At Turun Lyseo School, 40 teachers work about 30 hours each week and usually teach two different subjects. Students are required to take two of the following language courses: Latin, French, German, Russian, Swedish, or English. Computer lessons on an IMC computer and other models are offered once a week. The school's sports teacher, Raima Koski, was planning to come to Honolulu in December 1990 with ten others to participate in the Honolulu Marathon.

In the city of Porvoo, the teenagers' school had classrooms with televisions and overhead projectors. There was also a computer room for the 300 students. A company in Utah contracted with a Japanese firm to make these computers that were utilized in Finland.

A special Finn is the man, Arje Scheinin, who was the first Scandinavian to receive the International Dental Miller cash prize (1987). He discovered that xylitol found in birch trees prevents cavities. The chemical is now available in chewing gum throughout Finland.

While in Finland, I also met Jennifer Pelton from Oregon. Susan Griffith's book, *Work Your Way Around the World*, inspired Jennifer to apply here to teach English to two classes and help kindergarten teachers for one year. Jennifer's degree was in journalism. She saw a university notice about such a position and is now one of 800 from all over the world being paid to work in the Finnish

Foreign Trainee Program. Perhaps getting used to the winter daylight hours of 11 a.m. to 4 p.m. is the hardest part of the job.

Finland is known for its modern glass shopping centers, its new science park, preservation of old wooden buildings built above the two-to-ten foot stone foundations, and weekly saunas. Travels are smoother everywhere if you remember to start your question with hello, and end it with thank you. Here, hello in Finnish sounds like Hay Hay, and thanks is Key Toes!

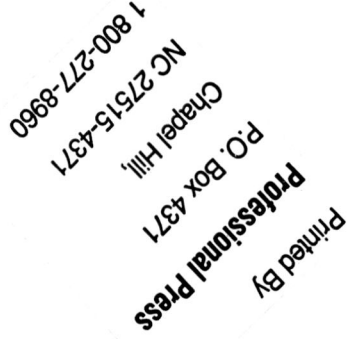

Printed By
Professional Press
P.O. Box 4371
Chapel Hill,
NC 27515-4371
1 800-277-8960

St. Petersburg, Russia

(formerly Leningrad, USSR)
September 7, 1990

The former Union of Soviet Socialist Republics occupied one sixth of the earth's land area. This former country was the largest in the world and contained fifteen republics with more than 130 ethnic groups. Since I visited St. Petersburg when it was still known as Leningrad, I refer to the city using its former name.

Traveling to Leningrad was a four-day bus tour from Finland. A visa could be obtained in Helsinki, Finland's capital. There was usually a seven day wait. The busload of 30 paid about $1000 each. The ride took one day.

While still in Finland, I paid $100 extra for a tour to a city school in Leningrad for students ages 4 to 19. An Intourist female guide met our bus at around 1:15 that afternoon and took me to a gymnasium where the Director of Foreign Affairs of Culture along with his wife and two young sons met me at the school door. They left after introducing me to the principal.

My Intourist guide and an office administrator led the tour through the school building. The school houses 1000 students with 92 teachers.

1990 saw many changes in the Soviet Union's educational system. Schools have more independence. Many gyms are specializing in science, music, and literature.

This school building is located across the street from an art museum. Plans called for grades 1, 7 and 10 to work with the museum staff. This had already increased the class size from 25 to 37. Another major change was the reintroduction of Bible lessons in the curriculum for grades 10 and 11. Greek mythology and Latin are introduced in grade 7.

The school term was from September 1 to May 31 with two weeks of summer school required for those repeating a course. Upper grade students had gone on a week's excursion to Moscow and Kiev for cultural programs. They also have weekend tent camping activities. Students in grades 10 and 11 walk to another school once each week for several hours of computer lessons.

In their classrooms, students sit in rows of desks and wear dark blue uniforms. In a geography class, eight small globes were used in group work. The teacher was utilizing a world map and showing slides when I entered the classroom. Student progress is reported in diary books which parents are required to sign indicating that they have read the report. English classes begin with two lessons weekly in grade 1. Classes begin at 8 a.m. and usually end at 2 p.m. Since there is some overcrowding, classes are also held in the small library. Parents are involved in cleaning and painting the school.

Special schools have been established for special education students. Kindergarteners ages 4 to 6 come at 8 a.m. and stay until 6 p.m. Nap time lasts from 1 to 3 p.m. in a room full of little wooden beds. Each of the kindergartener groups has a teacher, 2 part-time aides, and 18 children. Dancing, painting, music and daily walks are part of this program. After I had photographed the classes at the school, I gave a bar of English soap and an Earth space sticker to each of the teachers. Some of the older students gave me a piece of chocolate and their Lenin pins.

The principal is a former math teacher. She spent two hours with me touring the school. Afterwards we went back to her office for tea and questions. I commented on the many lovely flowers in her office. She told me that students bring them to her at the beginning of school. I was surprised when she gave me six pink roses from her desk. I later gave them to my Intourist guide.

All that one could buy with Russian rubles were postage stamps and post cards at the hotel. One ruble equated to 7 Finnish marcs and 1 Finnish marc equaled 28¢. Street sellers would accept hard currency (Finnish or American) for their Gorbachev dolls, jewelry, painting, wood art, fur caps, and embroidered aprons. Long lines of people were waiting to purchase liquor and cigarettes. In June, food ration cards had been issued. Cans of meat, jars of cabbage, and four-inch squares of some unknown food were available in one of the main stores.

Our guide told us that one third of the 5,000,000 inhabitants of Leningrad were pensioners. The waiting period for housing was 15 years. Housing, itself, cost 20 rubles per month for two small rooms. Wages were running between 150-250 rubles monthly then. There were very few people or cars on the streets.

The czar's summer palace is located in Leningrad. It was bombed during World War II, but it has been elegantly restored. The Hermitage Art Museum has famous collections here from all over Europe and from Asia. It would take ten years to see everything if one allowed only 30 seconds to view each piece displayed.

There was a great deal of discussion about changing the city's name back to its original name, St. Petersburg. Since the city was founded by Peter the Great in 1703, it was known as St. Petersburg from 1712 to 1914. It was then renamed Petrograd from 1914 to 1924. However, since Peter was a czar, the Bolsheviks believed that Lenin's pseudonym was more appropriate a name for this historical city and thus became Leningrad in 1925.

Sweden

September 12, 1990

S weden ranks first in the world for the lowest overall
student-teacher ratio, 18:1. The country ranks second in government expenditures for education
(Qatar is first).

Stockholm, Sweden's capital, is a modern city that
covers some 14 islands. It has many attractive old buildings, boats of all sizes, and a subway that allows you to
easily visit the sites in the area. City parks are geared for
the care of preschoolers. Couples are allowed one year's
vacation from work with pay. Schedules of such time off
are flexible. Many Swedish couples take the time together
to develop the parent-child bond. While I sat in one of
these lovely parks that was about 100 yards wide by 400
yards long, I noticed that many men were watching their
two-year-old children play with hockey sticks, climb a
model full-size truck, and pull city equipment wagons.

At the Maria Rektorsomrade Elementary School, the
basement was being converted this September to December into a bomb shelter. Heavy metal plates were placed
on the outside windows. I was unable to reach the

planning director to ascertain any more details about this project. The school director at Maria Rektorsomrade told me that there were 40 teachers serving about 400 students. Only three of the teachers were male. One teacher followed her students from grade 1 through to grade 3. Special teachers were hired to teach art, music, and sports. No religious classes were held in the school.

There were about 145 foreign students from 31 different countries that attended this school. The state provided two hours a week in one's native language. These special people came into the classroom to assist. The students are kept in a preparation class all day to learn Swedish and their basic lessons. No written reports were sent home to parents. Two parent conferences were held each year. Sixth grade teachers usually verbally inform seventh grade teachers about the students that would be moving up to grade 7 during a day in May. Special education students would attend another school. Parents assist with excursions, school plays, and garden activities.

School hours run from 8 a.m. to 2 p.m. The school term runs from mid-August to May 31. All students in grades 3 through 9 are required to take classes in sewing and woodcarving. Knitting sweaters, using a sewing machine, and carving small items are basic activities.

This school had a separate administration for students aged 7 to 18 who come during and after school for music courses. 1990 would see the advent of school decentralization to result in less rules and guidelines for operation. 1991 was set to change the form of financing of education by moving the liability from the federal government to local governments and communities with the safeguard that should a community be unable to meet all the needed expenses, the federal government would step in and cover the difference.

Compulsory military service exists for all men between the ages of 18 and 26. Military testing begins at age 17. The length of service depends on the scores students make on these examinations. Duration of service can be either 7.5, 10, 12, or 15 months. Women can volunteer for the service. Entry into the military can be delayed if one is attending the free universities, or if one is on an exchange program.

One family here has been hosting exchange students. Their sons were both in Australia through the auspices of the Rotary International Club program.

The border town of Helsingborg is a 20-minute ferry ride from Denmark. In this city of 25,000, there is a McDonald's restaurant that serves chocolate doughnuts. The youth hostel here is a villa on a hill with paths leading through a forest. The lovely home is used for a television room, a reception room, and serves a breakfast for $7 extra. The city bought this property and leases it to the youth hostel group. I spent the night alone in a six-bed cottage for only $16 as opposed to staying in a local hotel which would have cost $120.

The next night, a Danish engineer soon to be employed in Sweden and an American typist working in Switzerland made the evening discussion quite interesting in this women's cottage. Stockholm has the use of a ship docked near a museum for a hostel which is a most popular lodging spot.

One thing I have found in my travels is that museums have become the best places to see the treasures of other countries. When I was in Norway, I saw 72 costumed dolls on loan from the Soviet Union. East Germany had a great collection of Egyptian artifacts. Sweden has many Belgian wall tapestries. Items have often been purchased, donated, stolen, or taken as part of the benefits of an invasion.

A thought-provoking poster ad concerning spending money appeared while I was in Sweden. Its caption read: "This spacecraft took three people to the moon in 1969; this aircraft took 4.2 million people to the sun in 1989— Turkish Airlines."

In the city of Boden, above the Arctic Circle, I was surprised to turn on television at 7 p.m. and find the program, *Magnum P.I.*, (about Hawaii) in English.

Western Berlin, Germany

September 18, 1990

W est Berlin has a population of 2.1 million people. East Berlin has 1.2 million. Since 1961, the city had been separated by a four-meter high wall. In November 1989, tools and equipment were used to break down the eight-inch thick concrete slabs with rounded tops and once electrified barbed-wire fence. Pieces of the colorful graffiti on the west side of the wall were being sold for 60¢ an inch. Tourist buses arrived daily to look at the remains of this physical and psychological barrier. In spite of the publicity, some local people had still not taken the time, the subway, or the trains to visit their East Berlin neighbors with 45 years of Russian influence or to see the museum treasures of Germany's history.

A *Grundschule* near the center of West Berlin had about 420 students aged 7 to 12. Some of these students came from a Greek and Turkish heritage. There were two groups of preschoolers aged 5 and 6 with 15 in each class. The preschoolers' lessons ran from 9-11:30 a.m. A typical regular student's class day would run from 8 a.m. to 1:20 p.m. with about 25 students in each class.

English, French, or Latin lessons begin in grade 5. Art, German, music, history, sports, and technics (science) are also introduced into the curriculum around this time. The school year runs from September to mid-June. This particular *grundschule* was known for its successful sports teams.

Parents may elect to have their children have extra lessons after school. There were only five men out of a staff of 34. This number included an art teacher, a music teacher, and two sports teachers. Report cards are sent home twice yearly with a six-point rating scale where a rating of 1 is best. No homework is assigned to lower grades and no more than one hour a day is assigned for the older students. This school had no computers, though many of its students had computers at home. Computer school classes usually begin in a student's sophomore year.

Primary teachers keep the same students for either two or four years. Parents help with baking classes in the lower grades. They are also invited to a Christmas musical presentation though the school had no auditorium. Lunch time is not a part of the class day. Students may buy juice and eat sandwiches brought from home during the two daily breaks. After school, Greek students wait in the playground until their ethnic school meets in some of the public school classrooms in the afternoons from 2:30 to 5. The school's sixth graders were on a two-week youth hostel excursion up to the North Sea.

About six staff meetings are held yearly. There were no meetings between schools. Teachers have the option of taking two weeks away from the school year with pay for learning activities. Last year, ten teachers from several schools in the area went to England in May to study the English school system and gain practice in speaking English by living with families.

One entryway into the school building was beside the class gardens. Across the street on two sides were public parks. Nearby was a stylized fork monument dedicated to the memory of the air drops of food in the 40's. Berlin has been, is, and always shall be a modern, major city in Germany.

Eastern Berlin, Germany

September 20, 1990

1990 was definitely the year of tourism in Europe. Many people were visiting Berlin to see examples of a centralized economy compared to the profit market. This was made possible because of the collapse of the Berlin Wall in November 1989. It took about three months for most of the concrete barrier to be demolished.

In July 1990 the former East Germans could exchange their currency for West German Marks. October 3 was the date that the terms East and West disappeared from the name of Germany as the nation would reunite after 45 years. An interesting poster provided by Stuyvesant Cigarettes read, "Come Together and learn to live as friends!"

Europe has long been aware of the practical energy and achievements of the Germans. It will be another accomplishment to see how quickly the two groups can work together to modernize the entire nation. I wish I had thought about asking people if they considered themselves Germans or Soviets. (I think they would have said Germans!) Also in regard to unification—how long will it take for one side to become true citizens of the rest of the country? Will the new rulers see and accept any of the useful achievements of the past leadership?

While I was in East Berlin, I met a Brazilian and his German wife. They were asked to pay $130 for an entry visa to live in East Germany. They had come to Berlin instead. It is easy to tour both parts of the city by way of a local sightseeing bus or one can take a subway ride for about $2. I even took a ride to the end of the line so as to be outside of Berlin, but then I got on the wrong bus and rode back through areas of 12-story apartments in East Berlin.

At a comprehensive school here in East Berlin, I was able to visit with 10th graders learning English. Their teacher was recently involved in one of the first groups brought to California to practice English for four weeks.

On the *S Banhof* train, I chatted with a Russian pilot stationed near the border. He had taught his three-year-old son to read. His wife was a dentist, but she made little money. A Dutch physician told me that doctors and dentists in the Soviet Union were primarily women and were paid very little.

Alexanderplatz Square has a public cafe and observation floor in the television tower which is one of the tallest buildings in Europe. Another nearby 12-story building is called the House for Teachers. It was built in 1965. Yoga and jazz classes were listed on the entry board. The second floor had a public dining room with two of the five staff being English speakers. Buses from Poland could be seen in the area bringing tourists to purchase electronic products. Many tables were set up on the sidewalks to sell food, plastic products, and clothing.

In only a minute, the train crossed from West Berlin to East Berlin. I got off and walked to a market where a chubby man was wearing a green apron with the Del Monte logo on it. He and another man told me that there were no schools in the area. I showed another person my note written in German (by the hotel clerk) stating that I would like to see a gymnasium or Oberschule. I then asked some day care workers in a park and was, at last, able to locate (with hand signal directions) a nearby school that had been built three years prior to my visit. Next to it was an empty building that looked like nothing had been done to it since the 1940s bombings that destroyed nearly 70% of the city.

The female director of the school had her financial director, a man, give me a tour of the school. This school housed about 400 students in grades 1 through 9. There was a staff of about 30 people. There was no library or computer room. It was the first school to have a sports room. The room was located on the fifth floor. Below this room was another large unwalled room that was also utilized for sports.

Many classrooms had overhead projectors, screens, moveable vertical chalkboards, sinks, coat hooks, and cupboards. I saw a room full of hard frame beds for first graders to use when they took naps.

My tour guide left me in a classroom of fifth graders who were learning to speak English using pictures, cassette dialogue tapes, a wall map of England, and songs. The students had brought in photos of themselves to practice dialogue using the words: who's that, that is, she, he, and I. Students copied the dialogue from the chalkboard for practice as the teacher had the only textbook.

I was impressed with this same teacher's eighth graders who were able to ask me questions. I also asked about after-school activities and found that skateboarding was very popular after school. Students would also go shopping in West Berlin for watches, food, walkman sets, and clothing. History books were no longer being used at this school. Teachers and other workers here were concerned about losing their jobs as the quality of company products and information being taught was outdated.

School classes began at 7:30 a.m. and ran until 1:30 p.m. with a one-hour lunch break. Language classes in French, German, Russian, and English along with physical education were held in the afternoons from 2:30 to 3:15. For some, an eighth class period lesson was held until 4 p.m. English was at one time first taught in grade 7, but now it was being taught to fifth graders. Special language schools would start foreign languages in third grade.

Teachers normally have two subjects to teach during the year which runs from September through June. They taught 20 lessons per week. One of the teachers, Uta, had fourteen lessons per week as she also went to other schools to observe and guide other teachers of English. At this school, Uta taught German to ninth graders and English to students in grades 5, 8, and 9. In July, Uta and other English teachers were involved in a special program living with families in England.

There was no set policy concerning homework. There was considerable discussion concerning its validity. Parents were given a school progress report to sign in February and July. Field trips to villages in the Soviet

Union had been taken as well. Students utilized the schools there for sleeping quarters.

It seems that negative learning proceeds very quickly, even here in Berlin, as I watched a group of teenagers paint graffiti on a mailbox. I am certain that the world will be watching carefully the social and material changes in this newly united Berlin.

Bedford, England
October 15, 1990

Many people rush through big cities without noticing special historical sites and points of interest along the way. The world-famous White Cliffs of Dover are just one such point of interest on the journey across the Pas de Calais (or English Channel) to England. I rode a ferry out of Belgium for the four-hour journey. The Dover Castle is also near those famous cliffs and is famous for its old tunnels which were opened to the public in 1985. An old Roman homesite with painted walls was another discovery in the area.

Only a half-hour bus ride west of Dover is the Eurotunnel Corporation's exhibition. Local businesses and the local county education department have hired teachers to lead workshops about the newly constructed tunnel and to provide learning materials in both French and English. Videos and publications for ages 5 through 16 are available by writing to Eurotunnel Information Center, Tontine Street, Folkstone, Kent, England CT201 JHR. The Eurotunnel is a fifty-mile tube cut under the channel and through the chalk marl. It is expected to greatly enhance travel between Great Britain and the European continent.

North of Britain's capital city, London, are two very famous university cities — Oxford and Cambridge. Both universities house about 30 independent colleges, but degrees are awarded through the aegis of the city university. Lectures are seldom given. Instead, students meet individually with tutors for direction. Most of these colleges became co-educational in the seventies.

About 74,000 people live in the city of Bedford which is a one-hour's train ride north of London. This was the home of John Bunyan, author of the famous *Pilgrim's Progress*. It was also the home of John Howard, a man noted for his prison reforms. Commercial vehicles that bear the name, "Bedford," on the front grill are seen internationally. This is because Vauxhall Motors, Ltd., is in the Bedfordshire area and is wholly owned by General Motors in the United States.

Public schools in England would be considered private schools in the United States as fees are often collected to cover boarding costs. Bedford is rather unusual in that it has ten public British Independent Schools which serve about 6000 students. This includes four schools that are operated by former resident and ex-mayor of London, a Mr. Harpur.

The Mark Rutherford School in Bedford is ranked among the top ten schools academically in England. The school serves students aged 13 to 19. It is one of four state schools in the area. There about 1000 students and a staff of 60. The school term runs from September to mid-July. Classes begin at 8:30 a.m. and end at 3:45 p.m. daily. Snacks are eaten at the 11 a.m. break and a cafeteria lunch is served at 1 p.m.

Sports activities often take place during the lunch hour and/or after the regular school day. Students are involved in international rowing, volleyball, and judo competitions. Field trips are also taken regularly for studies in geography, history, and biology and involve journeys to Austria, Italy, and France. Parents are usually involved in fund raising, social activities, and teacher-friends' meetings. The head teacher is assisted with an office staff and three deputies who teach as well as monitor time schedules, perform counseling duties, and form a liaison between the community and nearby industries.

Roughly 15% of the student body is not from the local area as many students opt to attend this famous school which has served Bedfordshire for over 20 years. Students may leave the school system once they reach the age of 16 in England. Four years ago, only 27% chose to remain in school. In 1989, 55% elected to continue here. Government funding is available to schools. The amount of aid is tied directly to the student's age and the number of students enrolled.

Additional student funding is available from local industries through special initiative pilot programs. Business funding has made the purchase of Acorn, BBC, and Epson computers possible. It has also helped the school to develop special courses, to retrain teachers, and to hire substitutes during this training period. History, mathematics, science, and English classes also utilize the computers.

Upon entry into the Mark Rutherford School, the age 13 students are required to take French and German classes. Usually class attendance numbers around 20. The next year, they can elect to continue with one or both languages. By the time they are 16, Italian is offered in the curriculum, and students may then opt not to wear the black and white uniform. Homework assignments vary from one to three hours nightly. Religious education covering many different beliefs and value systems is taught in the humanities courses. Art, drama, and music classes are also offered. All ninth year students are bused to another location for swimming lessons.

Special aspects of the school include a part-time media trained person, a full-time youth worker as a liaison between community-school sports/interest clubs, and adults who are allowed to join in the daytime classes. A preschool play group utilizes one classroom until about 12:30 p.m. After that, the room is utilized as a dining room. The public library in the town shopping center rents out its lecture room three mornings a week to a children's play group.

The Education Reform Act of 1988 introduced a national curriculum for children aged 5 through 16 that was operative only in the state schools of England and Wales. The ten foundation subjects required by the act are English, mathematics, science, technology and design, history, geography, music, art, physical education, and for students aged 11-16, a modern foreign language.

Local newspapers have cited some of England's serious educational problems that have arisen from the lack of nursery educational opportunities for children aged 3 and 4. They also cited a low percentage of the gross national product being spent on education (6%—Canada spends 7.4%, the U.S. spends 6%), poor teaching, and the failure to properly educate the 40% of the student population that is not enrolled in academics.

Teacher recruitment programs have been started in Germany, Netherlands, and the United States to help England fill the instructors' positions that have opened because of chronic losses o£ local teachers due to low morale, social status, and lower salaries. Teacher workloads were increased with the enactment of the national curriculum which also stipulated that a testing program be implemented to evaluate student knowledge at ages 7, 11, 14, and 16. Often the ratio of primary students to teachers is about 30:1.

The current government of Britain has been moving schools in the direction of working with businesses and into competition. Roughly two-thirds of the teachers belong to one of three unions. Five years ago, a one-day demonstration was staged, but there have been no strikes.

1990 was the year for local communities to begin a taking over of financial management of the schools. This would also include the assignment of salaries and building care and maintenance.

A plaque at the London Design Museum reads: "The design of toys reflects the concerns and priorities of society and how it chooses to shape and influence child development."

Stratford-On-Avon, England

October 20, 1990

Double-decker buses haul tourists by the thousands past the 30,000 residents of Stratford (straight road) on (the river) Avon to access the five local properties that are associated with William Shakespeare, the famous actor and playwright of some 37 dramas and comedies. These plays are presented annually from April to January in this town which is located three hours northwest of London. Educational posters and ideas for teaching Shakespeare are available through the local Royal Shakespeare Company.

Shakespeare's grammar school (for boys) stressed the study of classical authors and Latin. At 13, he left school as his father could no longer afford the expense. Thus, Shakespeare was unable to study at the nearby university towns of Oxford or Cambridge.

This same school in 1945 radically changed its approach to education. Boys aged 11 to 18 were accepted, fees were abolished, and students were not allowed to board at the school. Today, the five core subjects offered are English, French, mathematics, religious instruction, and physical education. The 400 students have access to a drama stage, swimming pool, and technology center. April 23 was Shakespeare's birthday, and, ironically, the day he died. That date is commemorated annually with student flower processions in the town of Stratford.

Stratford also offers other spots of interest—in particular, its Butterfly Farm. Two brothers that operated similar farms in Florida and Switzerland started this greenhouse enclosure in 1986. The challenges of operation involve getting the food plants and flowers to bloom at the right time while maintaining a constant surveillance of temperature and humidity. Inside the greenhouses, one is greeted by yellow ginger blossoms, birds of paradise, periwinkles, hibiscus, and lantanas. Lily pads grow to nearly five feet across in the carp pond.

Students also enjoy an area at the Butterfly Farm known as Insect City. This section offers close-up viewing of the imperial scorpion, ants, bees, spiders, and the Mexican red-knee tarantula. The walls in the exit area of Insect City are adorned with students' two-dimensional drawings of beetles and written reports from Hollywood School in Birmingham.

Stratford's setting is truly English pastoral. There is something soothing about watching fluffy sheep chomping in the autumn drizzle at the edge of town. Nearby is Warwick Castle with rooms containing knights' armor and Blenheim Palace which is the birthplace of Sir Winston Churchill. Shakespeare was born, and died in this city. Today, there is a six-year-old Safeway store that serves 16,500 customers each week in its 19,420 square-foot building. The Stratford Marina boathouse rents out 30' to 70' houseboats for the week or a weekend to cruise the canal through the nearby locks.

The Teddy Bear Museum has a 6' standing Scot Guard bear at its entrance. On the second floor of the museum is a background painting and model bears with a picnic scene complete with bird songs. Also on display are a 1913 bear attached to a purse, a 1955 Russian bear with a balalaika instrument, a 1908 German teddy bear muff, and a 1950 Japanese bear who can flick the pages of a book. Teddy bear exhibits are presented in the Civic Hall during the months of February and July. A photograph indicates that the Rotary Club of Seven Oaks donates teddy bears to be carried in police cars for distressed children. In Honolulu, KNDI radio station sponsored the international magazine, Good Bears of the World.

Kenya, East Africa
October 30, 1990

Most visitors to this English-speaking country in 1988 were British and Germans (677,000 of them) who provided the mainstay of foreign revenues. Two-week tours from Manchester, England, or Frankfurt, Germany, start at $2000 and include either a three, four or seven-day safari. Near the Mombasa airport is a ten-minute ferry ride with local people and vehicles. It is a good starting place to learn about bargaining for quality carvings, wall hangings, cashews and jewelry. A chartered bus continues for about an hour's drive to various modern hotels and cottage-style lodges. Colorful local materials, Western shirts, dresses and trousers cling in the heat to the country sellers and town shoppers.

Square homes made of caked mud, stone chunks and poles are thatched with peaked roofs which provide protection from the equatorial sun. Shades of blue sky appear between huge clumps of white cumulus clouds with gray bottoms. One can also experience the beauty of the distant low hills, the feel of the light breezes, the chattering of crickets, the smell of burning grass, salt ash, the taste of bottled water with daily malaria tablets, the touch of flies patiently resting on your limbs, and watching tubes of dust being blown across the plains.

A safari van holds eight tourists who can shoot the safe wild game from the open sections of the van's roof. On this particular safari during a rest stop, ten elephants calmly walked between two vans that were parked only 25' apart. Varieties of deer stared at us wonderingly as we stared back with the aid of binoculars. Brown and black-striped zebras as well as rust-colored elephants and rust-colored tourists find the blowing dust and dirt churned up from the tires bouncing along the rough roads an effective camouflage. Lines of migrating wildebeests, sleeping lions, cheetahs with blood-smeared faces, giraffe heads above the trees, and black-brown deer-like topis were all within 30 yards of the camera-clicking tourists. Sparkling blue birds interrupted the quietness with sharp chirping. Policemen with guns man the tire spiked roads and check for poachers on the routes to view these animals. Since 1973, licenses to kill big game are no longer issued because of the abuse. Today, the 25 national parks and 23 game reserves focus one's attention on the harmony of wildlife and nature.

Kenya had a population of 21 million in 1986. The average family had eight children. The population is expected to double from the 1979 count by the year 2000. The unemployment rate is over 50%. Cucumbers, tomatoes, potatoes, rice, beef, fish and fruit are cultivated locally. Tea and coffee are significant exports. The year round temperature range is 75 to 95°F with high humidity. East Africa is an important center for members of the

Baha'i faith. The religious make-up of the area consists of 25% Christian, 6% Muslim and a few Hindu settlers brought over by the British to build railroads.

In Kenya, the KANU (Kenya African National Union), founded in 1960, has been the only legal political party since 1982. In September 1988, Daniel Arap Moi, who had been politically active since 1978, became the president of Kenya. The nation became independent from Britain in 1963. Kenya still receives military assistance from Britain as well as the United States who use port and onshore facilities.

According to the Europa World Year Book 1990, the educational sector of Kenya was allotted 19% of the total provisional budget for 1988-89. Kenya's school enrollment has increased by 73% between 1963 and 1988. Education is not compulsory; however, schooling begins at age six for eight years of primary education followed by four years of secondary education. The four national universities had a combined enrollment of 28,600 in 1988. One of the local English-language newspapers, Daily Nation (which sold for 3¢), stated, "Parents have been reminded that it is their duty to provide textbooks, houses, and other amenities to schools. The government will now be providing teachers to secondary schools. Cooperation between parents and teachers is necessary."

A visit to a village ten minutes from our Italian-built, Indian owned hotel revealed a hundred children clamoring for our limited sweet treats. The village's nursery school consisted of one totally barren room with barred windows. Across a dirt path, the two-room primary school was under construction. It was being built of limestone rectangles that cost 40¢ each. A bag of cement for a meter-square area cost about 60¢. The two-year teacher training would require an up-front amount of $2000. Many families cannot send their children to school as they do not have the money required for books and the school uniform.

A typical country state school was a seven-mile taxi ride on a dirt road from our south coast hotel on the Indian Ocean. About half of the 500 students were girls. Students begin school at age 7 in a cycle of three terms per year with three-week breaks in April and August and a six-week break in mid-November. Classes start at 8 a.m. and last until 12:30 p.m. for grades one to three. The upper primary grades return at 2 p.m. and remain until 3:45 p.m. Sports activities begin soon after and last until 5 p.m. Only a few rooms have desks. Four children are seated at each desk with approximately 50 students in each room. A battery-operated radio offers a variety of government sponsored lessons. The curriculum includes debate, writing, English and Swahili, science and agriculture, arts and crafts, mathematics, geography and civics, music, religious instruction of Islam and Christianity, and games. A wall chalkboard is the only other object in the room. The 1988 Swahili textbook was published in Nairobi, the Kenyan capital. The textbook contained no pictures. The English text came from the Progressive Peak English course booklets which were printed in 1988 with pictures. The friendly, quiet students greet with the popular expression, Jambo Rafiki, which is Swahili for Hello Friend.

Report cards are sent home at the end of each term. They must be returned signed to the school. Teachers are paid more according to their college test scores and by high ratings in instruction. Students were usually well-behaved and waited patiently in the humidity under coconut trees.

The Oxfam organization is one of the groups that is trying to create jobs and better earnings for craftspeople in third world nations such as Kenya. One of the educational units that they supply is the Gender and Development Unit which draws attention to the vital role that women play in the development of a nation. Oxfam draws its revenues from the direct importation of crafts and sales of those crafts through local outlets and mail order. These revenues are then used to help support projects in Asia, Latin America, and Africa. Oxfam's slogan is quite succinct, "A Donation Won't Hurt You."

Bedford, Ohio, USA
November 13, 1990

The educational history of Bedford, Ohio, began in 1878 when 241 students started school in this village located about 20 miles south of Cleveland. The district today includes four communities located in a 25 mile radius which is served by about 50 school bus routes. In 1982, the five member local board of education adopted a plan for integrating the Black students who make up about 40% of the total student population throughout the six schools in the system. Two of these six schools, have pupils only in Kindergarten, and grades 1 & 2. Two intermediate schools serve grades 3 through 5. The middle school instruct grades 6 through 8.

The 1275 students who are in grades 9-12 have classes that begin at 7:45 a.m. and last until 2:20 p.m. There is a professional staff of about 100. The enrollment 20 years ago was more than 700 students. At that time, only grades 10 to 12 were utilizing the school's facilities which include an Olympic-size swimming pool, a weight room, track ovals, tennis courts, and three baseball fields. Athletics are a primary part of the school program with interscholastic competition available in volleyball, wrestling, basketball, cross country, golf, football, and, a new addition in 1990, soccer. These programs are offered in three separate time slots of 3-5:30 p.m., 6-8 p.m., and 7:30-9 p.m. There appears to be no teacher shortage in this area. Salaries range from $23,000 to $50,000 annually. About 90% of the teachers are members of the Ohio Education Union. Community voters approve or disapprove three-year operating levies and bond issues for building construction and maintenance.

The Federal law forbids religious education in public classrooms. Ohio state requirements for graduation are: 4 units English, 3 social studies, 1 American history, 1 world history, 2 mathematics, and one-half unit of health and physical education. Eight elective units are also required.

The vocational-technical program offers courses in cosmetology, auto body repair and mechanics, and tool and die operation. Four years of foreign language courses are offered as electives. Selections include French, German, and Spanish. About 68% of the graduating senior classes continue their education. Few overnight excursions are planned except for individual or small group competitions in word processing, quiz programs, and a Chrysler Corporation sponsored class in auto (repair) troubleshooting. Community service projects by students include assistance at the elementary school until 3:30 p.m., writing letters to American servicemen, and visits to senior citizen nursing homes.

The school year begins at the end of August and ends the first week of June. The year is divided into four terms of nine weeks each. Report cards are sent home at the end of each nine-week period. There is no official homework requirement, although most classes assign it on a regular basis in the upper grades. The military is allowed to set up tables in the hallways that display potential benefits attained by joining the armed services upon graduation. About 25 parents form an advisory group to the system; however, no fund raising activities have been planned by this group.

In 1974 the state legislature of Ohio created a state lottery with some of the profits designated for education. Bedford High School receives about $100,000 yearly from this lottery which is used to purchase computer room items not included in the annual $22 million local district budget.

The newly elected Ohio Governor wants to initiate a state takeover of the Cleveland Public School System. He cites the ongoing problems arising from substandard housing (slums), Poverty, drug abuse, and racism which undermine the educational process. Ohio has 738 local boards of education elected by the local populace- The Cleveland area was once known as "the best location in the nation." This city has an "emerald necklace" of parks that almost surrounds this former steel-manufacturing center. The National Park Service administers the Bedford Reservation with its hiking trails, steam locomotive train ride, campfire ranger programs, and the locks of the once-famous Ohio-Erie Canal. The state is famous for giving the nation eight presidents and having unique Indian burial mounds.

Georgetown, Texas, USA

December 6, 1990

"Grate the rind of a Seville orange..." for pudding, states an 1832 cookbook that is in the museum collection at South Western University, the oldest area educational institution in Texas. One of the original, eight-foot-long classroom benches can be seen here with two attached right-handed writing desks. In 1888, the Ladies' Annex of South Western University granted Mistress of Literature degrees. Today about 55% of the 800 students at this school are women. The state of Texas was independent for nine years before gaining statehood in 1845. Texas became the 28th star on the American flag.

Georgetown is about 25 miles north of Austin, the capital of the state which is near the geographic center of Texas. Georgetown Independent High School serves about 1400 students in grades 9 through 12 from 8:45 a.m. to 3:45 p.m. Some 40 buses pick up students from the outlying areas of the district. Younger pupils arrive and depart the school one hour earlier. There is one building for kindergarten students, two buildings each for grades 1 and 2, grades 3 and 4, and grades 5 and 6.

All Texas public schools are independent of the state taxing system. and rely on locally assessed property taxes for funding. This results in a few communities having very little money for education. Ironically, in 1989, the Texas supreme court ruled that this public education funding system was unconstitutional. Changes must be initiated as per court direction by Ann Richards, the newly elected Governor of Texas, who was once a schoolteacher.

Teachers unions are not supported by the local populations in the state. Faculty salaries range from $18,000 to $30,000 per year. A recently created state lottery may be able to help with additional funding from education-designated funds.

Georgetown Independent High School has three assistant principals, three counselors, and an office staff of six. Teachers are required to attend a four-day in-service training seminar prior to the late August beginning classes. There are about 125 teachers. The school year ends in late May.

In order for students to graduate, the state of Texas requires that they have four years of English, three years of science and math, and additional credits in economics, government, and health/physical education. About 75% of the students participate in non-mandatory classes of foreign languages. Latin and German are offered in two-year programs: French and Spanish are offered for three-year programs. Other classes include auto mechanics, building trades, welding, and agriculture classes as well as an honors program in mathematics, history, science, and English. Roughly 55% of the graduating seniors continue studying at colleges and universities. About 20% will take further vocational training.

International Business Machines (IBM) set up a 20-computer lab at the high school free of charge for one year. The school later purchased the equipment to add it to its 3 other laboratories. The school has no official homework policy; however it is usually assigned on a more-or-less daily basis

State law requires that report cards be signed by a parent or guardian and returned to the school. Another state law requires that students must attend a minimum of 80 days per semester in order to receive class credit. Students wishing to attain drivers' licenses at 16 must prove that they have attended school the required 80 days the previous semester.

The license can be revoked until the student reaches age 18 if he or she is not In school.

Georgetown Independent High School has had the honor of having its band among the top ten ranked in Texas since 1982. A speech therapist, health testers, and a teacher for blind students are a part of the school's resource staff.

Autumn sports include football for the boys and volleyball for the girls as well as participation in other extracurricular activities. Participation in any extracurricular athletic program or activity requires passing grades. A swimming team utilizes a nearby college's swimming pool.

Spring sports include soccer, tennis, golf, track and field events.

In 1991, an alternative education program is planned to serve students from grade 8 to adults from 8 a.m. to 9 p.m. The program will include two full-time teachers. Students will also be able to contract from two to four hours of computer class instruction.

In 1990, a volunteer program with a start-up group of 70 adults had been organized to help teachers with breaks, counseling, attendance monitoring, workroom activities and bulletin board tasks. In addition, they could present lectures.

Over the last six years, Georgetown has hosted a speech and drama forensics festival that brings in some 800 students statewide. The festival begins at 7 a.m. and runs to midnight.

Saturday schooling is available for students with high absenteeism to make up the lost days. It is also used for students who have excessive tardiness slips and in certain cases of discipline. It is used for students in grades 7 to 12.

The student handbook is an important publication at Georgetown. A letter from the superintendent of schools which must be signed by parents and student, and must be returned to the school acknowledging that they have read the information. Of interest is a "new" rule that appears in the 1990 edition of the book that states that gum chewing is no longer allowed in the buildings. The handbook also contains considerable information covering school expectations, behavior, discipline, personal grooming, and the student council.

Short drives from Georgetown will take you to the Alamo in San Antonio, Austin's riverwalk (and San Antonio's, too), the San Marcos safari and cave, Houston's NASA Space Center, and Galveston's gulf beaches. It all starts..."deep in the heart of Texas."

Monterrey, Mexico
December 10, 1990

A one-hour flight from Houston Intercontinental Airport in Texas brought our plane to the balmy 65°F weather of Monterrey in December. The city lies about 144 miles south of the United States border and mountains with unusual peaks surround the plains. There are over 4 million inhabitants here along with considerable industries. Travelers visiting Monterrey will hear about the internationally famous Garcia Caves and the Institute of Technology.

Mexico has 34 states. The state in which Monterrey resides, Nuevo Leon, has 51 municipalities—and each has its own library. The local state governor has had these libraries constructed in just the last four years. Ten itinerant librarians travel throughout Nuevo Leon instructing potential librarians and patrons in card cataloguing and supervisory skills. The city of Monterrey has some 200 libraries.

The *Bibliotica Central* Library in Monterrey has a Commodore computer teacher who instructs ninety-minute classes from 9 a.m. to 7:30 p.m. daily. There are 10 students in each class. The teacher utilizes Mexican cartridges specifically designed for this instruction. Last year, about 1600 students took advantage of this opportunity to learn writing and other basic skills.

Primary public schools in Mexico serve students aged 6 to 12. The secondary schools have students ranging in age from 12 to 15. At *Escuela Secundaria, Numero Cinco,* founded in 1955, 75 teachers (68 women and 7 men) work with some 1200 students. The school year runs from August 20 to July 10. Five secretaries and five janitors assist with their respective duties from 7:30 a.m. to 12:30 p.m. Another team of students and staff utilize the school from 1 to 6 p.m.

The curriculum includes Spanish, English, mathematics, science (biology, chemistry, physics), social studies, art, music, IBM computer technology, and vocational orientation. Many students pay for private lessons in music and English. Almost all graduating students continue their education. The school offers adult education classes in the evening.

Have you ever heard of a fast-food chain known as, "Tortas Hawaii?" This chain serves a delicious sandwich that contains avocado, grilled ham and cheese, and pineapple in a special size of 5" x 3". I hope the chain comes to the Sandwich Islands (Hawaii)!

Vancouver,
British Columbia

(Canada)
December 20, 1990

The 1986 World's Fair silver globe landmark in Vancouver is now the Science World hands-on center and features /"Blue Planet," an environmental action film shown in the Omnimax theatre.

The city of Vancouver holds one's attention readily with its snowcapped peaks, harbors of oriental ships, and the town's bikeable seawall around Stanley Park. *The Vancouver Child* newspaper is a parent's guide to daily events held for children throughout the month, such as a children's film festival and the Imagination Market drop-in workshop.

In July 1867, England allowed the unification of northern North America which became the Dominion of Canada, the second largest country in area in the world. In 1931, Canada gained autonomy from Great Britain with total independence occurring in 1982.

The King George Secondary School is named for George V of England who lived from 1865-1936. The school is located ten blocks west of the downtown area, and celebrated its 75th anniversary in 1990. The school year begins in September and ends in June. There are about 400 students in grades 8 through 12 in these comprehensive classes. Class times are from 8:50 a.m. to 3:15 p.m.

Of the 400 students about 54% of them speak another language as their first language. Students in the district come from 34 ethnic backgrounds that include Viet Nam, Poland, Iran, China, United States, Philippines, Taiwan, Romania, Hong Kong, Czechoslovakia, and several countries in Central America. There are five Native American students. The English-as-a-Second-Language program has experienced a 50% increase in enrollment since 1987 and is in need of government funds. Students are immersed in the ESL classes the first year with 5 special teachers

About 37% of the students commute to school from a radius of about 20 km (12.5 mi). About half have part-time jobs and about a fifth will continue their education.

King George Secondary School has seven basketball teams. Practices for these teams as well as volleyball, soccer, softball, badminton, and tennis are scheduled during the day from 7 a.m. to 7 p.m. Night games are scheduled in the school-community gymnasium.

Courses offered at the secondary school include technical studies (metallurgy, woodworking, drafting, construction), home economics (textiles, clothing, nutrition, foods), English, art, science, mathematics, physical education, social studies, and business education. French is required for two years and offered for an additional two years of study. One laboratory has 30 IBM computers equipped with 15 printers. The school has no set home-work policy but does offer guidelines about assignments.

The student handbook has some interesting informa-tion in it. Of note are the following items: "If you don't use the library often, you are not getting your share of the tax dollars spent on-your education...Report cards to parents will be issued in November, March, and June and will indicate progress, work habits, and attendance...Some of the study skills that King George teachers feel are impor-tant are organization, time management, concentration, note taking, report preparation and presentation, test taking, reading, memory, critical thinking, motivation, and listening."

Special features at King George include an open bound-ary entry system (over 70% of the students are refused enrollment during the family interview). An international Visa program allows families from virtually anywhere in the world to pay for their child's attendance at King George— this program is responsible so far for the addi-tion of some 14 students. Names of King George's honor students since 1915 adorn the wall plaques that hang on the brick columns at the entranceway. The original brick column of the 1892 school also adorns the entrance.

An alternative "city school" in a nearby three-story building has 36 students in grades 9 through 12 with two teachers and an assistant to cover the curriculum. This school also utilizes city excursions as part of its educa-tional program.

The district has special programs and schools that serve students with learning disabilities. However, there is a growing teacher shortage in Canada because of low pay.

Home schooling has increased since the passage of the 1989 School Bill Act. Students must still be registered in a school of the parents' choice to take examinations. Vancouver also has a regional correspondence school center. Administrators are transferred about every five years to other schools in the district.

King George Secondary School also connects to the 11-year-old West End Community Centre. One simply walks through the large orange doors to gain access to two libraries, meeting rooms, pottery studios, photography studios, a theatre auditorium, saunas, squash and racquetball courts, an exercise room, a gymnasium, an ice skating rink, and a restaurant. Community centre membership is about $6 for adults and $3 for children each year. The winter program lists many activities for youths at an additional charge—preschool classes, parent-tot playtime, short videos, hockey, karate, swimming, exercise classes, piano lessons, guitar lessons, ballet, flute lessons, painting, After School Club, Kids Klay Time, birthday bash, teen mini sports tournament, weight workouts, and video with popcorn. The public library has been open Sundays for the past 18 years! No wonder the community centre membership was 11,000 in 1989. As one enters the gymnasium from the street entrance, there is a sign which reads, "Writing and graffiti on the walls do not fit our clean and safe image. Excessive noise and horseplay are not appreciated."

Up the street from King George School you can get Maui Ribs, California sushi, Peruvian mangoes, and "death by chocolate" cookies. These are just the right ingredients to get me back home to Honolulu to conclude a year of traveling around the world for education.

A Series Of Travelers' Prayers

Authors are unknown

Heavenly Father, look down on us, your humble tourist servants who are doomed to travel this earth taking photographs, mailing postcards, buying souvenirs, and walking around in drip-dry underwear.

We beseech You, Oh Lord, to see that our plane is not hijacked, our luggage is not lost, and our overweight baggage goes unnoticed. Protect us from surly and unscrupulous taxi drivers, avaricious porters, and unlicensed English-speaking guides.

Give us this day divine guidance in the selection of our hotels—that we may find our reservations honored, our rooms made up, and the hot water running from the correct tap, if at all. We pray that the telephone works, that the operator speaks our tongue, and that there is no telegram waiting from our children which would force us to cancel the rest of the trip.

Lead us, Dear Lord, to good, inexpensive restaurants where the food is superb, the waiters friendly, and the wine included in the price of the meal. Give us the wisdom to tip correctly in currencies we do not understand. Forgive us for undertipping out of ignorance and overtipping out of fear. Make the natives love us for what we are and not for what they can screw out of us.

Grant us the strength to visit the museums, cathedrals, palaces, and castles listed as "musts" in guidebooks, and, if per chance, we skip a historic monument to take a nap after lunch, have mercy on us for our flesh is weak.

For Husbands Only

Dear God, keep our wives from shopping sprees and protect them from bargains which they neither need nor can afford. Lead them not to temptation for they know not what they do.

For Wives Only

Almighty Father, keep our husbands from looking at foreign women and comparing them with us. Save them from making fools of themselves in cafes and nightclubs. Above all, please do not forgive them their trespasses for they know exactly what they do.

And Together

And, when our voyage is over and we return to our loved ones, grant us the favor of finding a willing audience for our movies and a sympathetic ear for our stories so that our lives as tourists shall not have been in vain.

Amen

Expenditures For Education By Country

The data appearing hereafter is excerpted from the UNESCO Statistical Yearbook 1989, table 4.1

During the eight years of the Iran-Iraq war, arms acquired by the two belligerents came from some 41 nations, 28 of which supplied both sides and accounted for 93% of the total weaponry.

Country	% of GNP spent on education		% Educ. Expenditure of total govt. expenditure	
Australia	1986	5.8	1986	12.6
Austria	1987	5.9	1987	7.8
Belgium	1987	5.1	1986	14.3
Brunei	1984	2.0	1982	9.6
Canada	1987	7.2	1987	15.4
China (PRC)	1985	2.7	1980	6.1
Costa Rica	1987	4.6	1987	21.6
Cuba	1986	6.6	1987	18.4
Denmark	1987	7.9	1987	14.5
Egypt	1987	5.5	1987	9.4
Finland	1986	5-9	1986	12.9
France	1986	5.7	1983	18.0
Germany (west)	1986	4.4	1986	9.2

Greece	1985	2.9	1985	7.5
Hong Kong	1984	2.8	1984	18.7
India	1986	3.4	1985	9.4
Indonesia	1981	2.0	1981	9.3
Iran	1980	7.2	1987	18.1
Iraq	1985	3.8	1987	6.4
Ireland	1986	7.1	1986	9.3
Israel	1985	6.8	1985	8.6
Italy	1986	4.0	1986	8.6
Japan	1986	5.0	1986	17.7
Kenya	1987	7.0	1987	22.7
Korea (south)	1987	4.2	1987	26.6
Kuwait	1987	5.3	1985	9.5
Lebanon	not available		1985	16.8
Luxembourg	1987	2.6	1983	14.1
Malaysia	1987	7.0	1985	16.3
Mexico	1987	3.4	1975	11.9
Netherlands	1985	6.8	1985	16.4
New Zealand	1987	5.5	1986	20.9
Norway	1986	6.8	1986	13.6
Philippines	1987	2.0	1984	7.0
Portugal	1987	4.5	1975	11.2
Saudi Arabia	1986	8.6	1987	13.6
Singapore	1987	3.8	1987	11.5
Spain	1987	3.2	1986	13.3
Sweden	1987	7.4	1g87	12.8
Switzerland	1987	4.8	1987	18.9
Thailand	1987	3.6	1987	17.9
United Kingdom	1986	5.0	1984	11.3
United States	1985	6.7	not available	

Memories of 1985

In January 1986, I invited friends to a potluck meal followed by highlighted comments of my adventure of six months around the world. There were times on that journey that I got tired of moving. In fact, after a month I remember not wanting to go out in the rain in Amsterdam to see another museum, but what drove me then and later was the thought of probably not visiting the area again.

Funny memories of the past now include: buying a French red portable typewriter and having the salesman take me to three Paris banks to get approval of my Master Charge card for the $300 sale. What an epic to carry that beauty; the worst part was having to learn a new order of French typing keys and then translating my notes when I ignored the system. The hotel clerk and I sat experimenting with the direction book at 11 PM in the lobby. Another incident humorous now but not then was on a tour to Agra, India. I asked the van guide if I could have one of the sodas sitting in view and he said no as they were for later use. I couldn't convince him to let me have mine now. I noticed others had brought their own bottled water. Thirst brings back another memory, this time from New Zealand where the mother of a young child shared her drink with me on the bus.

The European trains show up and disappear quickly. It was a challenge for me to board when no one was about or in the car; I never felt secure that I was on the correct train as no signs appear and trains move on various tracks within a few minutes of each other. I was always having dialog between my reasoning head and my feet which moved by intuition. My mind would be curious as to the day's adventure but my body would not want to leave the hotel. On the street, my mind would mention nervous ideas and want to return to security, but my feet would take my body and my mind on an exploration. Several times this occurred when I was not where I had planned to be, especially on the 1990 trip. Large cities in Italy were a maze to me with their circular lanes and no visible landmarks of varying height. I lost and found myself many times in one day. This solo traveling requires constant checking and planning but the advantage is knowing I can do so much more gallivanting about due to saving money by going without the tour costs.

My first Youth Hostel was a three-night stay in Cherbourg, France. I wanted to be there before the boat left for Ireland. This was one time the YH was very conveniently located which at the time was important as I had been hobbling about on a sprained right foot for the past month. Youth is in the mind, heart, energy and actions. If you're willing to have 2-20 people of the same sex in bunk beds in one room for the night, this $10 experience is for you. People of all ages and from various countries utilize this international lodging. It was great hearing about other people's experiences which they shared in the large community room.

I met a gal from Berlin who was also going to Ireland so we shared accommodations for the next 2 weeks in Ireland, Wales and Scotland in houses renting out bed/ breakfast accommodations. My regret is that I did not make and keep an address book of people I met. I did keep Sabine's address for a few years but never thought I'd get to meet her again.

On a train in Ireland, a woman invited me to stay with her in England, which I did about a month later. Two Australian women invited me to contact them on my arrival there. In Rome I shared the studio of a Malaysian fashion designer student. Each of these experiences enabled me to get away from hostels, hotels, and rooming spots to enjoy conversations about present and past travels.

An organization I wrote to before my journey was SERVAS, 11 John Street, New York, New York 10038, as they have host lists by countries of people willing to consider your staying with them free of charge. Their stationery states "open doors for travelers to homes and hearts in over 80 countries" and a quote from M. K. Gandhi "With every true friendship, we build more firmly the foundation on which the peace of the whole world rests." I did find a woman in Tasmania who welcomed me at a convenient time for both of us. It was a great way to get to know a local person and what's happening there.

Traveling alone helps one to become more open, spontaneous, outgoing, and risk taking.

This six-month adventure cost $12,000 including $2000 for train passes, $2,000 for the plane connections (SAS, Thai & United), $10 per day for meals, $16 for lodging,

$42 misc. daily expenses. In Europe, I met a woman from Hawaii who had a bag like mine who has been touring for ten years around the world!

Upon my return I sent a letter and copies of the photographs to the schools which I had visited. I wrote "I thank you for sharing your students and the school with me upon my visit last autumn. From August through December I visited 11 countries and saw much similarity in teaching styles plus classroom environments. I was impressed with small class size groupings, good discipline, and a concern for a pleasant learning environment. I was surprised to see so many children wearing school uniforms, no parent involvement, and little visible audio-visual classroom equipment. Now I too am involved with teaching. I work with about 70 Samoan children in groups of 8 for 20 minute periods. These kindergarten children come each day for language arts activities in a special program called Early Provision for School Success whereby we hope to target children needing the most help and offer some assistance to them upon entry into their schooling. (Since then the program was dissolved after five years and we support teachers have been sent back to self-contained classrooms— the system I started with over two decades ago.) It is still a lovely world in each city and country. It was my pleasure to journey and appreciate this experience by using some of my retirement funds."

Some famous quotes that pertain to a journey: Publilius Syrus: "No one knows what (s)he can do till (s)he tries." Eddie Rickenbacker: "Courage is doing what you're afraid to do." Martial: "A good (wo)man doubles the length of (her)his existence. To have lived so as to look back with pleasure is to have lived twice." Katherine Mansfield: "Risk, Risk. Care no more for the opinion of others or for those voices. Do the hardest thing on earth for you. Act for yourself. Face the truth." Thomas Huxley: "The great end of life is not knowledge, but action." And my quote to friends: "This is perhaps the biggest adventure of my life, and I'm brave and afraid moment after moment, even in the planning stages."

Other quotes but the source is not remembered. "Never forget you give but to yourself. Who understands what giving means must laugh at the idea of sacrifice." ..."As God sent me to you so will I send you to others. And I will go to them with you so we can teach them peace and union." ..."We must live as brothers and sisters or die as squabbling children." A Belgian Chef wrote these thoughts about his job: "Every day is different. I love the diversity and the challenge. Everyday is an adventure." That's how I would summarize this trip."

1985 Country Comments

France - Paris in July! The dream city of many Americans! I arrived alone and was intimidated by immigration procedures. I had the wrong form completed and when finished, exited again alone onto the street where I hailed a cab, showed him the written hotel address and looked forward to relaxing while waiting for my 5-week companion to arrive. We had planned to stay about 5 days per city, but Polly got an infected tooth so I was fortunate to be a tourist here for 12 days. Exciting surprises for me were: The Museum of Monuments containing reproductions of huge arches and sculptures, Les Invalides—a former hospital for 6000 and now an army museum (which made me wonder what a women's museum would contain), mastering the Metro subway with its 3 levels, and the underground tour of the sewers. The City Hall was a mammoth building with over 100 full figure sculptures on the outside walls. Eating dinner at outdoor cafes, overdosing on long loaves of French bread, and remembering the ceilings of the many rooms with the 173,000 treasures in the Louve remain strong memories.

So many "first" experiences—such as activating a 2-month Eurrail pass, hearing an organ concert in the Notre

Dame Cathedral, walking around the corner to see the glass tube escalators of the George Pump Exposition museum, going alone for the first time on a train to visit Fontaneaubleu Estates to see the English and French gardens, having a fantastic formal meal at Gare de Lyon train station, paying for a city tour and then falling asleep on the hot ride. Since many locals vacation during the summer, I thought the overburdened residents were friendly in their responses to tourists' routine questions.

Amsterdam - A pleasant six-hour train ride north of Paris. We chatted with a South African couple and a Greek family in our compartment. Canal boat rides and another train ride to Haarlem and a cheese market town made the country seem special. The home of Anne Frank had this information: "It was an era that demanded choice and then action: to collaborate or to resist; to stay or to flee; to protest or remain silent or; a choice in itself: to do nothing."

The following is a section from my own personal journal dated July 30, 1985. "10:30 AM. Rainy day in Amsterdam, Holland. I'm halfway around the world and tired of traveling since July 4th. Part of a book could be - Don't Go—because of hassles with weather, money, language, can't read signs, nor figure out maps or remember long street names. It's boring being a tourist—running from place to place. It's boring staying at home too—doing the same thing day after day with slight variations. So you can choose to spend a month-year-lifetime on a farm, city or address. Choose then to spice life with drugs or sex or whatever. Some find life bearable with a job or projects or a certain person or religious activity. Others who see themselves with no skills or talents or even interests or motivation also get to choose.

Perhaps we don't make specific choices at times like getting a limb amputated or having cancer, but our presence or actions allow us the possibility of those results. Allowing a government to draft you for overseas fighting allows you the choice of viewing that as an opportunity to see how the enemy lives and then choosing to follow orders to kill.

Alternatives are and are not apparent. Time provides more choices, but often decisions need to be made without the facts and delayed thinking. Often consulting with others results in yes or no viewpoints with few offering alternatives. How do we get to hear-see-feel-know the alternatives when it is so hard to communicate even with ourselves?

Change the view and what happens? Put new flowers in the vase and when do they stop being new? Just changing the water makes one aware again of them, but only for a brief time. Change the spouse or the house and when do you think of the old? Some action, sight, sound or thought triggers the memory computer; if you don't like it, repro-gram, cancel or escape.

My son once told me that he likes the sound of rain, so I recall that positive thought and wonder how he's doing miles away. It has stopped raining! I am also aware that this has been my first time alone in the hotel room in 17 days. I relish being by myself in my "home." Eating fruit & nuts and writing my thoughts seem more important right now than visiting a museum.

Looking at a picture of Gorbachev on *Newsweek* makes me recall Hitler and Hiroshima. What choices did people have during the war? Speak up against injustices and be tortured. Flee with your views. There is no where to run now with the nuclear situation. Few people take time to write letters or join the marches for peace. Perhaps the chores of making money to meet today's needs seem more important."

Every five years the tall ships and other vessels sail for a three-hour parade. Watching the Italian crew perched on the mast is still visible in my mind. Some boats are moving left while smaller ones are going right in the narrow passage. The colors, and shapes were a visual treat worth repeating. Trying to cope with street names eleven letters long made me look for landmarks instead of relying on letters. 2000 people on a summer day visit the Van Gogh Museum and 200 visit the Museum of Modern Art. The third museum made me want to write a story of riding horses through the gallery at night. This Rijksmuseum deserves a long visit!

Denmark - The 8 foot windows! The bottom pushed out while the top slanted in. Comforters on the bed became extremely hot to me in the middle of the night. I was lucky to be in town for a traveling circus with international entertainers. The circular stage allowed the audience to be no more than 40 feet from the performance. This country is a major gateway to the north; a second and longer visit for me occurred in 1990. Especially memorable was my first encounter with a button to flush the toilet and a shower drain on the bathroom floor, plus staying in a hotel room that had seven walls.

Norway - Still summer so schools are out of session. Polly had a SERVAS friend and went on ahead of me while I scouted for warmer clothes. Special sights in this country include the park of Vigeland's people sculptures, quiet dogs on trains, sod roofs, fiords, elongated waterfalls, a variety of cheeses and cold cuts for breakfast, pastel houses attached to each other, cobblestone streets, and wooden fences to block the snow.

Polly's friend planned a fantastic mountain bus trip for us to Sogndal, then aboard a boat to meet another ship. The connection timing was off, so we had to walk over a gangplank with our luggage in the middle of the lake to board the vessel. This memory excites certain nerves again! The many waterfalls seen on our way to Bergen and back to Oslo were so spectacular I deliberately planned to see that area again when figuring out my 1990 journey.

Switzerland - What a beautiful hilly, green, clean, tidy country! It is sectioned and influenced by the Germans, French and Italians. My parents had pictures taken in Geneva and Luzern enlarged and displayed in our family room for years. It was a treat to be able to see the real setting. Snow capped mountains in the summer attract many photographers.

Other Swiss events- $70 for two at a 4-star hotel where on TV we watched the Royal Hawaiian Band, information about the Big Island Parker Ranch, the Merry Monarch Festival of hula dancing in Hilo, and fifteen minutes of explanation about Hawaiian instruments—all without commercials! Train rides go through 91 tunnels! Thick comforters again—so I pulled out my gold aluminum foldable crinkly noisy sheet. Clothes and other items were left deliberately in hotels to make room for more needed objects or apparel.

Dula Public School, Luzern - September 3, 1985
    I obtained directions from the hotel clerk for the nearest elementary school. I could not locate the administration section of the three large buildings. I asked some boys about ten years who were playing nearby but they did not understand me. I walked in & knocked on the first door. The English speaking teacher invited me in to watch two student teachers working with her 16 pupils, age 4 1/2 to 6. Students were sitting in a semi-circle while the teacher talked and had the children raise their hands to answer and point to pictures on the floor. The children displayed quiet behavior on dismissal for free class play. The K room had a colored chalk mural done by the students. A 36" square graph was on the chalkboard, and pictures were on the backrests of the wooden chairs. I learned that the occupations of the parents of the pupils included photographer, hospital and hotel workers, police officers and psychologist. Families came from Spain, Portugal and Italy. Mothers stay home. There is little parent instruction involvement & no homework is given. The teacher writes a letter to the parents about 10 times a year. Parents are invited to breakfast and a barbeque with the class. Ms. Oahslin speaks German, Italian, French and English. She said there is a surplus of teachers. She had not heard of exchange teaching. Newcomers cannot get a government paper to stay and work. Most schools have one class per grade; this school has two K classes. The only resource

person is a dental hygienist. Teachers are paid by seniority and grade level. K teachers get the lowest salary.

The typical day is from 9 AM to 11:15 . Teachers and students go home for lunch. School resumes from I 30 to 3:30. Grade one lasts from 7:45 to 9:40, and resumes at 1:30. No films are shown in school. There is no alphabet study in Kindergarten. A child must be six by April 30 to enter grade one. The term begins August 20 for 6 weeks. The first two weeks in October are holidays with ten more vacation days for Christmas. They also have 2 weeks off for sports in February, and 2 weeks of vacation at Eastertime, plus six weeks off during July-August. Each canton (district) has a different schedule; some start in the spring. A child has to repeat a grade if she/he moves to another canton. On September 22 the people will vote on unifying the country's school dates. The schools pay for monthly excursions, papers and swimming sessions. Teachers are evaluated twice a year. A K inspector and a non-educator-political person come to do this.

Italy - Polly and I parted at a border town; she to return to Hawaii and I to venture on after 5 weeks of preparation for solo traveling under her guidance. When I returned to Honolulu 6 months later, I found that she had written about our time together. This seems to be a good spot for you the reader to see how her writings motivated me to keep a better journal on my next adventure.

"How wonderful it was! I was so very far from America. So much was very different, so much was universal. Here, on the other side of the world, people were walking these streets I had never dreamed of, eating food I haven't eaten, living in the midst of beauty I hadn't conceived. And now I have had the opportunity to touch buildings that were standing when America was discovered! Wonderful countries of Europe were mine to savor! Each day was an adventure; everything was different than what I had experienced before. It seemed my senses were on a constant "high", and how I relished it!"

Austria - August 27, Magistrat Der Stadt Wien (Vienna). I met Hans Kohut a former resident of Vienna who now resides in Israel. He became my guide and translator as we toured this training school for teachers as well as the community Kindergarten school. Teachers start the five-year training program at age fourteen. Presently there are 70 participants including three men. Instruction is in three parts: general knowledge, music/arts, and the study of children. The school year is the same as in the United States. 95% of eligible children go to nursery school. Pupils from the Philippines and Sri Lanka living in the neighborhood also attend here. Some Montessori ideas are adapted for use. A balanced curriculum is emphasized. English is studied beginning in grade three. There is no school nurse or health room; a sick child lies down in the class room. The only resource teacher is a religion teacher; parents can request that their child be exempted from the session.

A free quarterly state journal is given to the parents. The Principal, Dr. Hannah Fischer, had written an article about her trip to Hiroshima. Other articles were about health, children's journals, good toys, songs, & poems. Parents' meetings, discussion when pupils are dropped off, and communication continues at intervals. Philosophy for education is based on Katherine Reed's book "The Nursery School— A Human Relationship Laboratory." The parents pay for the nursery school - on a sliding scale. The state pays 50¢ per child. Teachers buy presents and supplies. Their salary is based on seniority.

Children must be six by August 30th to begin grade one. Some pupils arrive at 6:30 and can stay till 5:30. Others come from 9 to noon. Generally, instruction for Austrian children is from 8 to noon. There is no testing of normal children and no report cards. Teachers work 36 hours a week. Teachers are evaluated by the Director and only verbal comments are made. There was a special room for 19 children ages 2 and 3. In a classroom some children spoke German while playing with a toy train and blocks; some pupils were with the teacher and others active in small independent groups. Hallways had hooks for coats. Some classes have 25 pupils, a doll corner, home section with a stainless steel kitchen, a Black doll, no clutter or graffiti. Showers are available. All the children were well behaved and played quietly. Adults stand erect with heels touching and seem to maintain order by calm talks. Photos of the children were displayed by the main door of this ten year old building.

Ireland - St. Maries of the Isle National School, Cork, Eire, 9/13/85. The school term is September to June 30th with two weeks off at Christmas and one week at Easter. The new curriculum in the early 1970's emphasized group work. Age 4 pupils do pattern work, age 5 copy letters, and age 6 join the letters. Students age 4 and 5 are called Junior Infants and attend from 9 to 12:45. Age 5 and 6 pupils are Senior Infants with lessons from 1:30 to 3. There are 340 students in the school with 14 teachers including the principal who instructs remedial math and reading. Grade one students must be 6 by September 1 or repeat K work. If the parents work, a child may enter at age 4. Intercity enrollment dropped from a peak of 1400 to 340 because so many families have moved to the suburbs.

Schooling is free but parents pay for books. Local school money is raised by Sunday church collections plus fund raising through walks. There are no immigrants in this area; the Vietnamese are in Dublin. There is one Chinese family at the school. Progress reports are written on yellow paper at the end of the year for grade 2 and up. It is normal to allow students to continue their schooling without home funds. No provision has been made for gifted pupils.

No one in Ireland is allowed to divorce as it is not recognized by the state. 95% of the people are Catholic. The Department of Education supervises the Primary National Schools, often through the sisters and brothers of the church. Tests of achievement are given for entry into post primary or secondary schools or the community school.

The classrooms have wooden desks, very high ceilings, painted pink hallways, walled-in school grounds, and 11:00 chip snacks at recess on the asphalt courtyard. A booklet about the school and the area was given to me and other visitors.

Walking in the neighborhood, I saw a milkman collecting glass bottles from doorsteps. The temperature was 55°

in the afternoon. A vegetable stand posted signs stating the international location of the items, such as Irish tomatoes, New Zealand apples 15 pence, Italian peaches 10 p, So. African oranges 10 p, French peas 15 p.

Scotland - Findhorn Foundation, Forres, September 27

Members of this religious philosophical community pay about 200 pounds to participate and work there for a two year commitment. Some of the parents assist the educational committee. Ecology and harmony are emphasized. I saw a cabbage three feet in diameter, and still growing. There are 14 students in grades one and two. A pre-school is also available now with the hope of adding more grades each year. The Waldorf Steiner system is utilized in this communal setting.

The Royal Mile Primary Educational Institute ,October 4

This Edinburgh school begins August 20 through June 30. The typical day is 9 to 2:30. Some students go home for lunch while others bring a sack lunch. The Regional administration buys individually bottled milk, which is then free only for primary students. The parents of these 160 pupils are a mixture of unemployed, working class and University families. There is no classroom parent involvement other than with excursions. Parent donations of bakery items, games and home objects are used by the school to raise some funds to supplement the Region money for a rotating classroom computer. An interesting project is "sponsored silence," whereby adults pay children to work five minutes studying at their desks without interruption. The children wear ties in this litter-graffiti free school.

One of the primary (grade 1) classes I visited had 8 boys out of 22 students. The class was participating in movement exercises with the radio lesson. Another class was watching a TV program on values. A room off to the side was used for the storing of books, papers and coats. The bulletin board displayed Noah's Ark. Most of the teachers here are Protestant. Pictures for matching sounds and words are sent home each night. Conferences and written report cards occur twice a year.

There is a 13-point pay scale with an annual increase for the cost of living. Secondary teachers receive more pay. All contribute to the National Health Program. This school hires two special unit teachers plus two adult helpers to work with handicapped children. Some children are bussed here. After a trial period, if they are not able to join the normal class, they are sent elsewhere. One auxiliary teacher per school helps all teachers in the mornings. The head teacher writes comments to turn into officials, but does not observe teachers. The teacher's union wanted teachers to stop excursions and grading (considered non-teaching activities) but the teachers decided to do these activities as it would be more work later for them. The school looked immaculate; it had been painted this summer. The children looked neat in uniforms with ties.

Wales - October 4. The Adamsdown County Primary School in Cardiff is five years old & serves 136 students. Class size is 25-30 pupils with five full-time teachers. A part-time teacher helps slow students. The typical day is 8:55 to noon and then 1:30 to 3:30. Most students stay for free lunch. Students are in classes rather than grades. There is much visual stimulation on classroom walls and in the halls. School begins in September and continues to July 20 with one week vacation at Christmas and Easter. The year is divided into three terms with one week off during each term.

Teachers give spelling lists and paper booklets for children to read to parents at home. Two four-year old pupils brought their booklets to the head teacher (principal) to show Mrs. Rees how they had copied the teacher's writing and could read it. In the open, large classroom settings, the principal encourages the teachers to devote some time to each student for personal attention.

There is no parent involvement at this inner-city school. Written reports go home at the end of the year. Parent conferences are scheduled in November plus appointments which can be made during the year. Teachers get no written evaluations from officials; comments are made by the head teacher. The teacher gets a basic salary and extra payment for curriculum responsibilities. There is a two-year probation before salary increments are automatic.

This city on the southern coast has a castle which was occupied until the 1940's. It was one of the best I have ever seen! What a treat for these students and tourists to recall history with a walk to the castle!

India - October 18, 23. Several blocks from the Hotel Oberoi in Delhi is a government pre-school. I saw about 20 tots attending class from 9 to 1:30 with 2 teachers and an aid. Students sang a song and a 3 year-old became the leader with a strong voice. The room had little light and an area about 25' x 18' with a darker, smaller room off of that. I saw no supplies or furniture. Education is almost free and there are 30 centers which include lunch and mats with a small courtyard for play. Teachers seek donations and get 1/3 of the funds from government assistance. Many students were not in school that day, Oct. 23rd, as it is the culmination of a week's festival of "good prevails over evil."

Holy Child Heart Secondary & Primary Schools, Delhi
School construction began in 1973 with completion 3 years later. There are 2600 students, 100 teachers, 4 office staff, 4 lab workers, 11 cleaners, 2 gardeners plus canteen workers. This best girls' school is equivalent to St. Xavier with 1100 boys. The parents are in business occupations. There are many K-12 schools.

Most of the students are Hindi with 20% Christian. About 30 buses bring and return the pupils from 7:30 to 1:30. There is a 20-minute lunch at 10:45. Sixty students are in each class sitting two to a desk. Classes are from April to March. May 15 to July 15 students are home plus one week in October and one week at Christmas

Student leaders help with discipline, although all classes seemed extremely well behaved. Homework is done in school for one hour on Friday. The gifted can participate in sports, music, dance or art while the rest do homework or make class charts. Team work is encouraged for the benefit of the slower students. Some scholarships are given. Written reports are distributed. Students are taken to the theater. Science films are shown every three months. Some students have color TV at home. The first Saturday of each month parents meet with the teachers, and can also come during recess or lunch. Some teachers offer free community lessons to other students in the afternoons.

The students here get high scores. After class 12, about 25% go on for professional training, 75% to the University. 5% transfer in while the rest begin in grade one.

Lasting impressions of a five-day visit to Delhi and Agra include the multitude in white clothing, cattle in the streets, historic buildings, dryness, colorful saris, large hotels, walkers, and a special captivating charm which I am unable to put into words. A special treat for me was having Mr. Kanzwar, desk clerk at the Hotel Oberoi, take me to the above schools and then to visit his family for tea in his home.

Thailand - October 21. By visiting the YWCA in Bangkok I was able to join some women leaders as they taught songs and counting activities to young children who were locked up with their moms in a refugee center. Some people were there because they had no identification.

Mrs. Boonchuan Hongskrai, the Y's Executive Director, made arrangements for me to visit her daughter's private school about two blocks from the Y. Thienprasitsart School was built in 1973 for boys and girls age 3 to 6. Classes are from 9 to 2 with lunch and milk served. There are 8 classes with 40 pupils in each. The 3-year olds have two teachers and one helper. The school has a pool with a male instructor. Homework begins at age 4 on Monday, Wednesday and Friday. The older students have daily homework in English, Thai, and math. There are no films. Class activities observed were: music, writing, games, drawing, review of letters.

The school term is from May to October with a short break and then continues to May. This was the first day but it is usually in November. The Thai President wanted the children to have time off to see the December event games of football, gym, bowling, swimming and pingpong which is held every four years.

Parents do not help in the classroom but are given a monthly report. A blue school report card was given to me which showed the following subjects: reading in Thai, Thai Language, tell life experiences, Math, English, Skill in thinking, art, listen and follow directions, weight & height development, and Total Score.

About 90% of the Thais are Buddhists. Bangkok is a special city in that fantastic temples are enclosed in the center of town. Golden pointed roofs, taller than life statues and the close building of one temple to another leaves a desire to revisit (which I did), and revisit. Local tours for a day to the famous war area of the River Kwai and canal boat rides expand one's history.

Australia - October 30. Brisbane, my favorite city, probably because of its hills and a river in town. A few highlights from West End Infant School—215 pupils of which 67 have English as a Second Language. 43 were Greek, 39 Vietnamese, 15 Chinese, 10 Lebanese, 9 Aborigines 7 Kampuchean, 5 New Zealanders, 4 Turkish, 4 Fijian, 3 Indian, 2 Chilean, and one from 14 other countries. A staff of 9 plus 2 ESL teachers with 7 aids were going to go through an adjustment time as the leaders decided to drop the aids in favor of getting new computers. Kindergarteners come two days a week at age three. Pre-

School is 3 days a week at age 4. The Queensland schools are on a semester system starting the end of January to Easter for a 10 day break. Terms are in ten week blocks with a semester break. Teachers are paid the same no matter what grade, but seniority and degrees result in more pay. The first year teacher is sent to the bush country for experience. Report cards are sent home twice a year supplemented by parent conferences. Parents help supervise small groups, prepare classroom materials and assist with excursions. Inspectors come for first and second year. They look for current curriculum planning information on the desk and at other records, watch for 1/2 to 2 hours. Evaluation is given to the school, followed up by only oral comments by the Principal. The teacher's union offers medical and dental benefits. It is compulsory to join a medical plan; the hospital is free.

Crown Elementary School, Sydney — November 4
  This intercity school had many Chinese, some Greeks, Yugoslavians & Vietnamese to comprise 135 students with 6 staff, 2 ESL teachers, 1 craft leader and a part-time librarian. Most students bring home lunch and are there from 9:25 to 3:25. Time out areas are used for discipline. A Chinese resource teacher was teaching brush painting and moved to various classes. The Principal also had a class. One computer was used by different groups on various days. This is the first school playground I saw with painted circles for games.
  The Florence Sultman Kindergarten cute home around the corner from the above mentioned school was built in 1920 and owned by the Kindergarten Union which started

in the early 1900's. The K.U. has some schools open 50 weeks 8 - 5:30; there are also private and independent schools for these young learners. Two excursions are taken a year. Parents come and watch or cook special treats. This home had 25 students a day, some come for 2 days, others for 5 . The program is from 9 to 4. Teachers keep records on students but no reports to parents are given in writing. Low income or pension people pay $1 a day with the rest paid by the Dept. of Youth. The fee is $30 a week. I was quite impressed with the outdoor enclosed area of grass, climbing equipment, sand box and a tree house.

A train ride along the eastern coast of the continent shows various types of kangaroos, a wild purple flowering plant, the Blue Mountains with scenic one day tours to a revolving restaurant. Best of all is a flight to Tasmania where nine days is not enough time to visit by bus the special scenic towns.

New Zealand - Auckland, December 11. The typical day at Myers Kindergarten School is from 8:45 to 3:15 with an hour for lunch. Term one is from February to May with a 2 week break then, and resumes til August 16. After 3 weeks break school continues till December 13. The Kindergarten Association is the employer, but the teachers are paid by the government. Most classes have 35 pupils in the morning, 30 in the afternoon with two trained staff, and 1 full-time aide. 1986 was to see a unified education program under the Dept. of Education. Parents are encouraged to come and stay as often as they wish in the classroom. No report cards are given, but a trial run listing interests, and extra work needed may be started soon. Last year this school had 9 non-English speaking students.

The North and South Island are connected by a scenic cruise ship. Both islands should be visited, especially the cities of Rotorua with its sulfur steam vents along sidewalks and Queenstown with its skylift to food.

Author's Final Thoughts

People have asked me what places were the best. For me, during the 1985 adventure, I was impressed with Switzerland, Norway, Tasmania (the Australian island-state), and New Zealand. From the 1990 epic, I'd add the Lafoten Islands off Norway & the northern part of Norway & Sicily. What regrets do I have: the countries of Korea, Japan and the Philippines were not added to my information.

There is something special about solo adventures. One of the joys is the freedom of doing what you want when you want and how you want. There is also the satisfaction of handling challenges, self-discipline and responsibility. The major disadvantage is not having someone who enjoys hearing about your discoveries. Some of the key words relating to "Why travel?" are curiosity, discovery, newness, surprises, direct personal experiences, finding out for yourself. Adventures make people, history and events more meaningful. There is so much to remember! I recall stating "I will remember every day everything I see and do."

Considering the scientific changes and men's desire for power with money, I wonder what should be taught. Why is it the belief and willingness to go to war continues? What can be done to emphasize the needs of people and the dangers of weapons and conflicts? Do we educators serve a country's power leaders? Now with business becoming partners with educators and scientists in bio-technology, are we all losing sight of the value and the needs of the individual?

The Globe and Mail paper p. A 4, issue 12/20/90, stated:

"14 million children will die every year unless world leaders agree to spend as much to save them as they spend every 10 days on their military. Unicef said it will cost $20 billion a year for the next decade to reduce child deaths and malnutrition by a third as promised by world leaders at a UN summit on the world's children in September 1990. Two-thirds of the money must come from developing countries...Industrial nations must restructure their aid and focus on health and education."

John Wayne said "Old men should stop wars." The TWA in-flight magazine Dec. 1990 p. 69 stated: "Martial arts: to subdue the enemy without fighting is the highest skill." and "rhetoric - the act of finding the best available means of persuasion" and "language is the most powerful weapon we have." Perhaps with all our "tools" we can teach and learn how to care for one another and our planet.

School Addresses

These people may be able to help answer questions or direct you to other sources for personal or class correspondence.

The list includes schools from my 1985 travels, and are listed alphabetically by countries.

Australia

Gilles Street Primary School
Prin. Max Green
Gilles Street
Adelaide, So. Australia 5001

West End Infant School
Prin. Mr. Bliss
Hardgrave Road
West End
Brisbane, Queens, Aus. 4101

Ringwood Elem. School
Prin. Mr. Adamson
Greenwood Avenue
Melbourne, Victoria, Aus. 3134

Crown Elem. School
Prin. Marie Dolman
Crown Street
Sydney, NSW, Aus.

Florence Sulman Kindergarten
Tchr. Jan Norton
33A DenHam St.
Surrey Hills, NSW
Sydney, Australia 2010

Augusta School
18 Hildern
Tch. Cecily Westwood
New Town, Tasmania, Aus.

Austria

Hauptschule Wilten
Dir. Anton Triendel
Innsbruck, Austria

Buildungsanstalt for
    Kindergartnerinnen
Magistrat: Der Stadt Wien
Prin. Dr. Hannah Fischer
21 Patrizigasse 2
Vienna, Austria

Belgium

Stedelyke Municipal Adademie
   voor Schone for Fine Arts
Brugge, Belgium

Technich Institute
Tch. Odette Maerschand
Onze-Lieve-Vrouw
Tweebruggenstraat 55
Ghent, Belgium

Brunei

Sekolah Rendah Dato Godam
Hdm. Flj Mohammad Flj Tarih
Bandar Seri Begawan, Brunei

Canada

King George Secondary School
1755 Barclay Street
VP. John Crowe
Vancouver, BC, Canada V6G lK6

England

Butters Court County Primary
   School
Hdm. James Astbury
Beaconsfield, England

Mark Rutherford School
Head Tch. Mr. Brandon
Wentworth Drive
Bedford, England MK 418 PX

Big School
King Ed. VI Grammar School
Stratford-Upon-Avon, England

Germany

Grundschule
Tch. Angela Grunow
Alte Hellersdorfer Str. 22
(East) Berlin, Germany M52

21 Oberschule
Tch. Uta Jahns
Wilhelm Puch Str. 116
(East) Berlin, Germany 1040

Grundschule auf dem
   Tempelhofer Teld
VP Mrs. Gotze
Schulenburghing 7-11
(West) Berlin
1000 Berlin 42, Germany

Grundschule
Dir. Erau Muhlhahn
Schwanthaler Str. 87
Munich, Germany

Grundschule Primary School
Hauptschule Middle School
Oberammergau, Germany

Hong Kong

Peniel School & Kindergarten
90-98 Portland Street
Prin. Chu Lai Ming
Kowloon, Hong Kong

India

Hold Child Heart Secondary
   School
Hdm. Sr. Judith
Tagore Garden
New Delhi, India 110027

Indonesia

SD Negeri No. 015
Prin. Raja Zakaria
Tacon Raden Patah
Lubuk Baja
Batan, Indonesia

Ireland

Sr. Maries of the Isle National
   School
Cork, Ireland

Josephian Girls National Sc.
Prin. Sr. Ursula
61 Mount Joy Street
Dublin 7, Eire (Ireland)

Italy

Mazzini Scuole Elementari
Piozzale
Prin. Dr. Dusi
36061 Bassano Del Grappa (VI)
Italia

American Overseas School of
   Rome
Prin. Dr. Robert Silvetz
via Cassia 811
Rome, Italy 00189

Kenya

Kingwede Primary School
Box 35
Msambweni
Kenya, East Africa

Liechtenstein

PS Aule
Tch. Rudolf Schaedle
Giesseustrasse 14
9490 Vaduz, Liechtenstein

Malaysia

Sekolah RJK (c) St. Joseph
Sr. Asst. Mr. Wang Lok Keng
Jahore, Bahru, Malaysia

Mexico

Escundaria No. 5; Dr. R. Salinas
35 Anos de Fundacion
Monterrey, Mexico CP 64800

Simon de la Garcia Melo
Esc. Primaria
Dir. Roberto Salinas
Juarez y Tapia
Monterrey, Mexico CP 64000

New Zealand

Myers Kindergarten
Head Tchr. Jan Ahern
381 Queen Street
Auckland, New Zealand

Russia

Aehumefrag
yse Umncemefinoeg 3
Dir. Anna Kozhemjakuva
Ulukazuea nfill
Tocygopcmbenao ee
(Lenningrad)
St. Petersburg, USSR

Scotland

Royal Mlle Primary Educl.
Institute of Scotland
Prin. Miss Edwards
Cannongate,
Edinburg, Scotland

Findhorn Foundation
Forres, Scotland IV360TZ

Singapore

Singapore Life Presby. Church Sc.
Prin. Yvonne Foo
Singapore

Sweden

Maria Rektorsomrade
Dir. Anders Kallmodin
Rungvagen 23
11652 Stockholm, Sweden

Switzerland

Dula Public School
Tch. Isabelle Oahslin
Salistrade 18
6003 Luzern, Switzerland

Taiwan

Chung Sing Primary School
Tch. Percy Chiu
Taipei, Taiwan

Thailand

Thienprasitsart School
Dir. Mrs. Prajitra Thienprasit
6 Soi Attakarnprasit
Sathorn Tai Road
Yannoves,
Bangkok, Thailand 10120

USA

Bedford High School
Assoc. P. Mr. F. E. McNellie
481 Northfield Road
Bedford, Ohio 41146

Georgetown Independent
School District
Georgetown Independent High
Sch.
Georgetown, Texas 78628

Wales

Adamsdown County Primary
School
Prin. Mrs. M. J. Rees
Cardiff, Wales CF2 lJF

For additional copies, send $12.00 to:
Hands
52262 Chatam Court
Granger, Indiana 46530

Italy

Brugge, Belgium

India

Macau